Six Sigma
for Business Leaders

A Guide to Implementation

Gregory H. Watson

Business Systems Solutions, Inc.

GOAL/QPC
IMPROVING THE WAY ORGANIZATIONS RUN

First Edition

Six Sigma for Business Leaders: A Guide to Implementation

Cathy Kingery, *Editor*
Janet MacCausland, *Graphic Design and Layout*
Bob Page, *Project Manager*

GOAL/QPC
12 Manor Parkway, Salem, NH 03079
800.643.4316 or 603.890.8800
Fax: 603.870.9122
E-mail: service@goalqpc.com
MemoryJogger.org

Printed in the United States of America

First Edition   10 9 8 7 6 5 4 3 2

ISBN 978-1-57681-049-1

Acknowledgments

Our thanks and gratitude go to the people and organizations who offered encouragement and suggestions for this book or who gave us permission to incorporate their information to make this book a practical aid for business leaders.

We are indebted to the following reviewers who reviewed and critiqued draft copy to ensure that the book met their expectations: James Bossert and Duane A. Floyd, *Bank of America;* Larry Smith, *Ford Motor Company;* Linda Phillips, *Honeywell Corporation;* H. David Speer, *Maytag Company;* John H. Breckline, *Nokia Internet Communications.*

Special thanks to those deployment champions and Master Black Belts who have helped so much in the development of this material: Janet Young of *American Express;* Chuck Aubrey, formerly with *American Express* and *Sears;* Johnnie Davis of *Crane;* Steve Bailey and Don Lindsemann of *DuPont;* Tony Abraham, Ken Bushell, David Cox, Claude Pigeon, David Sims, Phil Vallance, and Aldous Wong of *Imperial Oil, Ltd.;* George Brazuk and Randy White of *Monsanto;* Timo Hannukainen and Simo Salminen of *Nokia Mobile Phones;* Catherine Johnson of *Noranda;* Jack West of *Northrup-Grumman* and *ASQ;* and Hitoche Otsooka of *Toshiba.*

Foreword

Six Sigma initiatives have spread from American industry across the globe as business leaders recognize that such initiatives can improve operational performance and help them to deliver their long-term business strategy. With this growing interest in Six Sigma, there has been an increasing demand for sound guidance regarding alternatives to consider for its implementation. A "one-size-fits-all" cookbook approach does not typically meet the needs of many senior business leaders, who instead prefer a customized version that is aligned with the organizational culture they have taken so long to establish.

In the mid-1990s, only a handful of consulting firms had any real-world experience in assisting business leaders in designing Six Sigma implementations. Today, hundreds of companies claim expertise in Six Sigma implementations. But the definition of "Six Sigma" changes considerably across these different organizations. In a move to standardize the meaning of Six Sigma, the American Society for Quality (ASQ) created a Body of Knowledge for Black Belts in an effort to proscribe the tools contained most frequently in successful Six Sigma training programs.

This fourth Six Sigma book from GOAL/QPC provides knowledge that is important for business leaders to understand and apply in their initiatives. To develop this book, GOAL/QPC partnered with Business Systems Solutions, Inc., to integrate their extensive experience in implementing Six Sigma with management teams in the Americas, Europe, and Asia. This partnership ensures that the information in this book is pragmatic and addresses the realistic concerns of business leaders considering implementation of Six Sigma.

Like all GOAL/QPC books, *Six Sigma for Business Leaders* is a practical text. It is intended to support leadership teams as they design their Six Sigma initiative and manage the execution of Six Sigma through aligning it with their business strategy. This book supports executive- and champion-level Six Sigma training for business leaders and process owners.

We believe that the insights contained in this book, which have been gathered from many sources, create a valuable resource for helping business leaders implement a successful Six Sigma initiative in their organization. We trust that you will agree.

Bob Page
GOAL/QPC

Contents

Appendices

Introduction

Six Sigma has become American industry's new strategy to increase profitability and enhance customer satisfaction. As a result of the pioneering work of Motorola, reinforced by further development at companies such as ABB, AlliedSignal (now Honeywell), DuPont, General Electric, and Toshiba, Six Sigma has become a recognized method of business improvement. Even senior company executives averse to other quality-management initiatives have embraced Six Sigma as a proven way to decrease costs, grow profit margins, increase market share, and improve customer satisfaction. Six Sigma helps organizations to be high quality, low cost, and lean in everything they do. Six Sigma supplements an organization's fundamental business processes in a way that ensures achievement of its long-term vision and objectives.

Although many of the tools associated with Six Sigma are not new, their implementation and deployment in this process are unique. Four specific aspects of Six Sigma are new or were not properly emphasized in past approaches to quality improvement: (1) integration of the human and process aspects of business improvement, (2) concentration on obtaining bottom-line results using structured methods that link analytical tools into an overall framework, (3) a standardized method for resolving chronic work problems, and (4) an integrated, phased approach to applying the problem-solving and analysis tools.

First, the human aspects of a Six Sigma initiative include operating with a sense of urgency to evaluate and correct problems, focusing on customer concerns, working in project teams, driving for bottom-line results, and emphasizing continuous improvement. The process aspects of a Six Sigma initiative include a disciplined approach to problems, dedication to process improvement, a focus on customer requirements, use of quantitative measures and methods for understanding sources of variation, application of statistical methods to establish performance parameters, and use of process management to sustain improvement gains. Six Sigma creates constancy of purpose in an organization by adding a new dimension to business-process measurement: variation as an indicator of process performance.

Second, management personnel in Six Sigma companies understand that their chief responsibility is to foster and encourage such improvement efforts. They do this by making the improvement of their companies' business processes and products/services a part of every employee's job, providing appropriate training at all levels of the organization, and making quality improvement a "competitive sport" by assigning the roles of champions and Black Belts to drive improvements.

Third, Six Sigma organizations conduct statistical problem solving that facilitates getting to the fundamental nature of a problem. They do this by using a five-step problem-solving process: Define, Measure, Analyze, Improve, and Control, or DMAIC. It is the principal responsibility of management to establish the business context for a Six Sigma change-management process. Only when management chooses projects that focus on improving the infrastructure of the organization's core business processes (i.e., those processes that provide competitive distinction) can significant gains be realized from a comprehensive Six Sigma improvement effort.

The Six Sigma improvement approach has a set of best practices associated with its implementation. This book summarizes these best practices and puts them into a context for senior management to use as a guideline for implementing Six Sigma in their organizations. It answers fifty questions that an organization must address to initiate, develop, and sustain a successful Six Sigma deployment. In answering these questions, it provides a coherent business-management process with practical suggestions for realizing the benefits of Six Sigma. This book is intended for top management teams of organizations that are either considering the deployment of Six Sigma or seeking to enhance the effectiveness of their existing Six Sigma initiative.

What is Six Sigma?

The phrase "Six Sigma" has taken on several different meanings. It is more of a business strategy than a quality program. To achieve the maximum benefit from a Six Sigma initiative, an organization should tie Six Sigma improvements to its corporate strategy and goals for business performance. Consider the following definitions of Six Sigma:

❑ **A philosophy of management.** As a philosophy for business operations, Six Sigma recognizes the direct linkage among numbers of product defects, wasted operating costs, and level of customer satisfaction with a company's goods and services. As an operating philosophy, Six Sigma provides a framework that ties together business improvement and quality initiatives and aligns an organization to goals that are evaluated by their productivity, cost-effectiveness, and quality. Six Sigma focuses on eliminating mistakes, waste, and rework using a measurable approach, statistical analysis methods, and alignment to organizational priorities to increase customer satisfaction and enhance the bottom line. The essence of Six Sigma is the scientific method applied to routine work processes.

❑ **A process-measurement methodology.** Six Sigma is a way to predict the probability that a process will produce results that meet customer expectations or stated requirements. Process sigma is the number of times that the process standard deviation can be divided into the difference between the process center and the closest specification limit that identifies the customer's tolerance for process variation. Standard deviation, a commonly used measure of variation, is represented by the Greek letter σ (sigma). Less process variation (i.e., lower standard deviation but higher process-sigma levels) means better process-performance consistency.

Using sigma as a common metric across processes permits the comparison of relative quality levels across similar and dissimilar products, services, and processes. The current competitive level of performance in business is in the range of three to four sigma. Many companies operate below this level. The sigma scale is exponential when translated into defects per million opportunities (DPMO). Performing at a one-sigma level means that a process is producing more defects than good results from an external customer's point of view.

▶ TIP

The sigma performance scale on the next page can be translated into measures of process capability for both Cp (design capability for potential process performance) and Cpk (capability for real-world performance). It can also be used to estimate the cost of poor quality at each level of sigma performance. Interpret the gap between Cp and Cpk as the potential performance improvement.

Sigma Performance Scale

Sigma Performance Level*	Defects per Million Opportunities (DPMO)	Process Yield	Process Capability (Cp)	Process Capability (Cpk)	Estimated Cost of Poor Quality (% Revenue)
1.0 σ	670,000	33%	Not capable	Not capable	>40%
2.0 σ	308,537	69.2%	Not capable	Not capable	30–40%
3.0 σ	66,807	93.32%	1.0	0.5	20–30%
4.0 σ	6,210	99.38%	1.33	0.83	15–20%
5.0 σ	233	99.9767%	1.67	1.17	10–15%
6.0 σ	3.4	99.99966%	2.0	1.5	<10%

* The numbers in this table were derived using the Six Sigma convention of applying a 1.5σ shift to the short-term value for sigma found in normal statistical distribution tables. For instance, the numerical value for 6σ taken directly from a statistical table would be 0.002 DPMO, but applying a heuristic value of 1.5σ to account for variation takes the process to 4.5σ (3.4 DPMO). It is more precise to calculate the difference between long- and short-term process performance than to use this heuristic.

❑ **An analysis methodology.** Six Sigma is also a disciplined, data-driven methodology for decision making using statistical analysis to amplify the effectiveness of an organization's best workers. This methodology combines a step-by-step analytical approach to problem solving with statistical tools used in a specific sequence to expose and control sources of variation to optimize process output.

- **Problem-solving process:** This is an evolution of the Plan-Do-Check-Act (PDCA) Cycle and focuses on the actions of the Black Belt working in conjunction with his/her managers. Called the DMAIC sequence, it consists of five steps—Define, Measure, Analyze, Improve, and Control—that are performed in two distinct phases: characterization and optimization. These five steps help to focus the problem-solving process. DMAIC is preceded by the Recognize step of the Six Sigma improvement process, which is the strategic consideration of what projects to conduct, and it is followed by the Standardize and Integrate steps, which implement the recommended improvements in the process.

- **Approach for innovation in product and process design:** This process, which combines characterization with innovation, is called DMADV. The five steps of this process are Define, Measure, Analyze, Design, and Verify. Like the DMAIC process, DMADV is preceded by the Recognize step and followed by the Standardize and Integrate steps. DMADV has three different implementation approaches: one for hardware products, one for software products, and a third for business-process reengineering.

❑ **A business culture.** Six Sigma is also a culture that motivates teams to work on a common problem to achieve higher levels of performance effectiveness and productivity at a lower cost. After an organization operates a Six Sigma program for about three years with top-down support, then management by fact, root-cause analysis, and definition of problems according to source of variation all become part of the organization's business language and form a common bond among employees at all levels. With their joint efforts, a long-term process for problem prevention and corrective action built around Six Sigma thinking and its action-oriented philosophy can be put into place.

CAUTION

Since the term *Six Sigma* has so many different meanings, management personnel must be clear when they announce that their organization is going to "do Six Sigma." They must operationally define key terms so members of the organization do not mistake management's intent or misinterpret the meaning of the message behind their words.

A Six Sigma improvement initiative contains both management and technical components. On the management side, it concentrates on finding the right process metrics and goals, as well as the right projects and the right people to work on them, and using management systems to complete the projects successfully and sustain gains over time.

On the technical side, it focuses on enhancing process performance (i.e., improving the average level of performance and reducing variation) using process data, statistical thinking and methods, and a disciplined approach to process-improvement methodology. This approach has four principal steps: measure, analyze, improve, and control. The statistical and quality-improvement tools are linked and sequenced in a way that is easy to use and effective in analysis. This approach focuses on the identification of the key process drivers (i.e., primary sources of variation) and relies on statistical software to simplify the calculations.

Six Sigma can be summarized as a business-improvement approach that seeks to find and eliminate causes of mistakes or defects in business and product-development processes by focusing on outputs that are significant to customers and on the inputs that affect those outputs. Process and product variations strongly affect product-production lead times, product and process costs, process yields, and customer satisfaction. One of the most important aspects of the work of a Six Sigma Black Belt is to define and measure variation, discover its causes, and develop efficient operational means to control and reduce it. Six Sigma features a rigorous problem-solving approach, the dedicated application of trained business analysts to well-structured process- or product-improvement projects, and the attention to bottom-line results and sustaining them over time.

▶ TIP

The time to challenge the structure of a Six Sigma initiative is when your organization first considers implementing one. Some of the areas to consider customizing include the following:

– The name of the initiative. Many organizations don't want to use the name "Six Sigma" because it looks like it belongs to another company and does not fit into their culture. A few interesting alternatives are Management Innovation, Accelerating Continuous Improvement, and Business Excellence.

– The titles used for Black Belts, Green Belts, and Master Black Belts. Many organizations find that these martial-arts-derived names do not fit into their culture and change them to better reflect their values or historical quality programs. Some options include Quality Expert, Process Engineer, and Change Agent.

– The role of the Green Belt. Companies implementing Six Sigma generally opt for one of two roles for Green Belts. In the first, the Green Belt is treated as a "junior Black Belt," working on projects with a toolkit similar to the DMAIC Black Belt toolkit, but their problems have a smaller scope and are chosen by their local managers.

In the second role, the Green Belt serves as an apprentice to a Black Belt. The primary role of the Green Belt in this role is to facilitate the application of analysis tools that involve close participation of front-line workers. Organizations that take this route typically desire to avoid overlap between the Green Belt and Black Belt roles and perceptions of their relative value to the organization based on the projects they conduct.

– The project-management structure surrounding Six Sigma. Many organizations find they already have in place some of the support infrastructure that is helpful in creating a successful Six Sigma initiative. They should review these business-management tools to ensure they support the Six Sigma initiative, but they should not develop a duplicate set of support tools.

▶ TIP

Management should describe a Six Sigma initiative in a way that is clear to the entire organization. It is helpful for all members of a management team to talk about Six Sigma using the same language and to have a common perspective on why it is important for the company. During the initial business-leader training, a workshop to develop an "elevator speech" might prove helpful. An elevator speech is a shared message used by the top management team to communicate the essence of a subject that is short enough to be discussed during a brief elevator ride. Develop no more than seven main points to communicate what Six Sigma is, why it is so important to your organization, why it is different from what you have done before, why it must be done now, and what the organization hopes to achieve by when.

A sample Six Sigma "elevator" speech

❏ We have achieved our current success by focusing on the continuous improvement of our business goals. We shall persist in this management philosophy.

❏ To continue improving our competitiveness and to achieve operational excellence in all dimensions of our work, we need to flawlessly execute the daily fundamentals of our business tasks.

❏ We have concluded that the Six Sigma methodology, with its disciplined approach and statistical toolkit, gives us the best potential to be cost effective in all our work and at the same time to meet the growing performance expectations of our customers and shareholders.

❏ This is the next logical step in our improvement program, and we are embracing Six Sigma to sharpen our analysis tools while focusing on eliminating defects and waste throughout our work processes.

❏ Achieving success in Six Sigma will require the involvement of all employees at all levels of the corporation: as project sponsors, process owners, project champions, Black Belts, Green Belts, or members of the team that supports the analysis and does the actual work to enable our success.

QUESTION

What makes Six Sigma successful?

Implementation of a Six Sigma initiative requires a fundamental shift in an organization's business approach. It also requires a cultural change that emphasizes continuous improvement, work measurement, management by fact, and accountability for results.

When an organization implements a Six Sigma program, its management style must shift. Many senior executives use "Theory O," which entails making experience-based decisions supported by assertions and anecdotal information without the benefit of objective facts and root-cause analysis. (See Question 26 for more information about Theory O.) A Six Sigma program requires management to replace this management style with fact-based, statistically supported thinking. The DMAIC and DMADV processes both help turn Theory O ideas into hypotheses to be tested using statistical methods. They allow management to objectively evaluate the credibility of long-held beliefs and ways of working.

The following tools and processes are critical success factors for managing the transition to a Six Sigma program.

❑ **Readiness assessment.** This management-level assessment is conducted to evaluate an organization's readiness for implementing Six Sigma. It concentrates on the organization's history of deploying improvement initiatives and the lessons learned from these experiences, the human resources system, the organizational culture, the Six Sigma–related skills and competence within the organization, and the ability of the organization to assimilate change.

❑ **Deployment plan.** This plan is an outcome of the readiness assessment. It identifies the proposed deployment sequence and performance milestones. It also addresses the education of senior business leaders, process owners, Green Belts, Black Belts, and Master Black Belts, as well as generic training for the organization. The deployment plan can also include the communication plan for the Six Sigma initiative.

❑ **Reward and recognition system.** It is important that the work of Black Belts and Six Sigma project teams be recognized for their valuable contribution to improving organizational performance. Human resource specialists and staff compensation managers should develop an appropriate reward and recognition system that is aligned with the culture of the organization and its compensation policies.

Other tools and processes that might prove helpful for large-scale corporate deployments of Six Sigma include the following:

- **Cultural alignment and program customization.** After the readiness assessment is conducted, the management team must evaluate how their organization's culture aligns with the expectations for a successful Six Sigma implementation. The culture of the organization and historical linkages to previous improvement initiatives should be integrated with the Six Sigma training program so employees perceive Six Sigma as a natural extension of previous improvement efforts.

- **Customer-requirements analysis.** The organization must conduct research to determine where it fails to either understand customer requirements or satisfy the level of performance they desire. This analysis is needed to ensure that critical-to-satisfaction (CTS) characteristics are identified and that Six Sigma projects can be aligned to the customers' requirements. Organizations can use quality function deployment (QFD) as a methodology to describe customer requirements and translate them into business actions.

- **Enterprise map.** This value-stream analysis describes the high-level operation of a business and how core business processes are broken down into work-level processes. Completion of an enterprise map makes such things as unnecessary feedback loops and long decision-authorization pathways more evident. Together with the business measurement system (described below), the enterprise map helps to identify projects for Black Belts by illustrating where performance gaps in the work-process flow are evident.

- **Business measurement system.** Business performance indicators ("business Y's" in the language of Six Sigma) that show excellence has been achieved from the point of view of the overall organization are identified and translated into work-process measures (e.g., quality, cost, and cycle time). This system identifies problems as well as new opportunities for improvement and is a key source for Six Sigma project ideas.

- **Strategic benchmarking of key performance indicators.** Benchmarking key business processes to understand the performance of the business Y's should be done using external validation of observed problems noted in the business measurement system. External comparisons help to validate current performance capabilities and establish where excellence exists while also serving as a valuable source for discovering new improvement ideas.

- **Business governance self-assessment.** A self-assessment using the criteria of the Malcolm Baldrige National Quality Award or the European Quality Award is a good way to identify opportunities for improvement. Gaps in performance between an organization's practices and the best practices outlined in these business models are a potential source for defining Six Sigma improvement projects.

- **Policy deployment planning system.** Policy deployment, also called hoshin kanri, provides a system to define an organization's strategic direction and then deploy its resources to achieve it, one project at a time. This planning and management system presents opportunities for defining Six Sigma projects that are fully aligned with the business's change-management strategy.

- ❑ **Quality-management system.** This is part of an organization's framework for business control and represents a means to deploy improvements from Six Sigma projects and ensure that they become part of the organization's routine operations.

- ❑ **Communication plan.** This describes what must be presented to the organization and the best channels for communicating it. This can include support mechanisms such as an intranet Web site for news, project information, and training materials. Other aspects of this plan include networking sessions among Black Belts and project champions, and annual internal meetings where Black Belts compete for "project of the year" or other recognitions.

- ❑ **Employee involvement.** Teamwork and employee involvement are essential aspects of Six Sigma projects. To reduce resistance to change and encourage a more positive working environment, the participation of those employees who will be implementing the change is essential. All Six Sigma projects are team projects. A collaborative work environment involving all the affected participants is essential for successful project work.

▶ TIP

The amount of work needed to develop a successful Six Sigma initiative often requires an organization to designate one or more individuals as deployment champions (see Question 13). These people are charged with evaluating and potentially modifying current organizational business-support systems or developing new ones to enable the success of the Six Sigma deployment. Deployment champions coordinate the development of a plan for implementing a Six Sigma change initiative for their entire organization. This is more effective than having an initiative that is just driven by top management.

To ensure the organization receives a message that is consistent with the executive sponsor's intent for doing Six Sigma, the deployment champion should also facilitate regular meetings of the organization's leadership team. The purpose of these meetings is to make decisions about strategic projects to be conducted, review strategic project progress, evaluate new ideas for implementation in the Six Sigma effort, and review completed Black Belt projects. Perhaps the most important job of the leadership team is to develop and integrate the Six Sigma tools and processes outlined above into the organization's normal management process. This will ensure that Six Sigma becomes part of the organization's regular way of working and not merely a level of bureaucracy layered upon basic business requirements.

How is Six Sigma different from other improvement initiatives?

For the past twenty or so years, business leaders have been besieged with various business-improvement initiatives. These include statistical process control, total quality management, just-in-time manufacturing, kaizen (continuous improvement), ISO 9000, business-excellence assessment, benchmarking, business-process reengineering, and the lean enterprise. Below is a summary of these improvement initiatives.

- ❑ **Quality circles and the seven basic tools.** The quality-circles movement trained teams of front-line workers in the basic analytical tools they needed to improve their own performance by using practices such as suggestion-and-reward systems. These teams not only analyzed their own processes and continuously improved them but also took on many of the basic management tasks of front-line managers. This allowed their supervisors to have a broader span of control.

- ❑ **Statistical process control (SPC).** This methodology is used to monitor the performance of any repetitive process. By collecting data at various points throughout the process in small samples, instantaneous average performance can be calculated and accumulated into an overall performance rating. The range of observations can be compared to the standard deviation in an effort to understand the variation under which the process operates. SPC is used to differentiate between special-cause variation (which is due to specific problems) and common-cause variation (which is designed into the inherent process capability).

- ❑ **Breakthrough management.** Joseph M. Juran initiated the emphasis on quality as a management methodology. Drawing an analogy between quality management and financial management, he developed the Juran Trilogy, which states that in both finance and quality there are three key processes: planning, control, and improvement. Juran also stated that two kinds of improvement help organizations succeed. Continuous improvement helps an organization that is the leader in its industry; breakthrough improvement helps an organization that is a follower and desires to be a leader.

- ❑ **Zero defects (ZD).** Philip B. Crosby, who created the concept of ZD, maintained that defects indicate lack of conformance to customer requirements and that any defect was unacceptable. Prior to that time, defects were an accepted way of life in industry; the objective was to minimize them to between 1% and 2.5% of the production size.

- **Total quality management (TQM).** Introduced in the U.S. during the early 1980s, TQM integrated many of the methods used in previous quality systems: teams and their basic analytical tools, SPC, customer-first thinking, and the total involvement of the organization in making improvement occur. TQM was the first comprehensive quality-management system that went beyond mere management of product quality to emphasizing the quality of the entire organization.

- **Just-in-time (JIT) manufacturing.** JIT focuses on managing production lots one product at a time—reducing cycle time, setup time, waiting time, and inventory throughout the whole system. JIT operates hand-in-hand with TQM because it puts the responsibility for work quality at the level where the work is performed and implements a work system that makes defects visible—not covered by layers of inventory, which tend to hide the real-time detection of problems.

- **Quality function deployment (QFD).** This methodology was developed to align the design of products and services with the needs of customers. It translates the "voice of the customer" into the "voice of the process" that will fulfill customer expectations. QFD is also a documentation-management tool for the product-development process because it tracks a product from its concept development to the point of readiness for full production.

- **Kaizen (continuous improvement).** Continuous improvement is both a business culture and a way to manage daily, routine business activities. It differentiates between in-process performance measures and results measures as a means to evaluate where process performance degrades.

- **ISO 9000.** The British Standards Institute (BSI) originally created a supplier quality-management standard (BS 5750) and presented it to the International Standards Organization (ISO) for consideration as a standard for the European Union. It was accepted and published in 1987 as ISO 9000. Two subsequent upgrades have moved this standard from its original intent to a broad definition of a quality-management system that can fit any business. ISO 9000 operationally defines a quality-management system and provides for third-party verification of performance. This third-party audit serves as a single evaluation point for an organization and is much more efficient than conducting individual evaluations for all of a supplier's customers.

- **Statistical engineering.** This method involves a set of basic statistical tools for conducting a variables search for the so-called Red X: the missing factor that drives variation in a process or product. The multi-vari tool and the "B vs. C" (before change versus after change) comparison help demonstrate where variation occurs in the process that is being improved. These methods are simplified to allow front-line workers to participate in the analysis process.

- **Design of experiments (DOE).** An analysis using DOE can optimize performance by determining which variables have the largest effect on a process outcome or product performance, determining set points for variables that have an important effect on a process, and establishing tolerance limits for the operating characteristics of a process.

- **Business-excellence assessment.** Two quality awards initially used by the American government to stimulate performance improvement were the NASA Lowe Award and the President's Award. The U. S. Senate Productivity Award was established for productivity improvement. A consortium of organizations then lobbied Congress and the White House to create a National Quality Award, which eventually found its administration under the National Institute for Science and Technology (NIST) and the American Society for Quality (ASQ). The Malcolm Baldrige National Quality Award Criteria, which provide an operational definition of TQM, can be used by the senior management of an organization as a self-assessment tool to determine where the organization has opportunities for improvement.

- **Benchmarking.** This is a process for comparing an organization's performance against that of others. Organizations can learn from the best practices of other companies how to improve their own performance.

- **Business-process reengineering (BPR).** This is a "clean sheet" design of an organization's key business processes as enabled by technology, primarily information technology.

- **The lean enterprise.** A system that emphasizes the improvement of quality by eliminating waste and reducing delays and total costs. It fosters an organizational culture in which all workers continually improve production processes and their skill levels.

What's not new?

Most of the tools and methods used in Six Sigma were developed over fifty years ago. Many Six Sigma projects, especially those that work on transactional business processes, do not require the more sophisticated tools. As with other improvement methods, improvements resulting from Six Sigma come one project at a time, and the total impact on an organization is a function of the implementation of project-specific improvements. Generally speaking, the more projects that an organization completes, the bigger the impact of a Six Sigma initiative will be on the organization. Finally, long-term success in doing Six Sigma requires the dedicated attention of business leaders, who must ensure it remains a visible initiative.

What is new?

Six Sigma is aligned with an organization's business objectives and holds business leaders accountable for the execution of improvement projects. Business leaders must prioritize these projects and act as management champions to facilitate their execution. A graduated skill pyramid of Green Belts, Black Belts, and Master Black Belts are assigned to be dedicated resources for projects and are held accountable for applying an organized, structured analysis toolkit (DMAIC) and personal computer tools (e.g., Minitab statistical software, Corel iGRAFX 2003 simulation software, and Microsoft Office) to seek solutions to chronic business problems.

❑ **Six Sigma vs. quality circles and the seven basic tools.** While quality circles focus on a bottom-up approach to quality improvement, Six Sigma takes a more dominant top-down approach to defining improvement projects. But project teams formed by Black Belts use the quality-circles methods and approach, and Green Belts and Black Belts use the seven basic tools.

❑ **Six Sigma vs. SPC.** SPC is an individual tool included in the QC toolkit. It is best used in combination with the seven basic tools for variables screening and should be used in conjunction with DOE for setting control points used in the SPC chart. Six Sigma includes SPC in the tool sequence to follow a variable screening process and DOE.

❑ **Six Sigma vs. breakthrough management.** Breakthrough management provides a set of principles to move an organization forward. Six Sigma incorporates these principles into its executive training programs and into the application of DMADV.

❑ **Six Sigma vs. ZD.** ZD provides a goal for an organization: flawless execution of its customers' requirements. Six Sigma incorporates that goal and quantifies progress toward that level of performance through the use of 6σ as a metric—one that can be used for both attribute (i.e., counted) and variable (i.e., measured) data.

❑ **Six Sigma vs. TQM.** While TQM makes improvement part of everybody's job, Six Sigma makes tackling the toughest problems the job of the Black Belt. TQM projects tend to come from the workplace, while Six Sigma projects tend to be aligned with business strategy. TQM uses a portfolio of tools with no fixed sequence of application, while Six Sigma has a rigorous, step-by-step learning sequence for applying almost exactly the same toolkit. While TQM uses "soft" costs (e.g., cost of poor quality) to measure problems, Six Sigma tracks savings to the bottom line.

❑ **Six Sigma vs. JIT manufacturing.** JIT focuses on work flow; it reduces defects and eliminates inventory that is not needed to produce a product. This emphasis on work-process control is included in the DMAIC Measure step as a means to establish the sources of defects and in the DMAIC Control step as a means to implement lasting improvements.

❑ **Six Sigma vs. QFD.** QFD is best used when technology is being adapted for use in a product or a process according to customers' requirements. Six Sigma employs QFD in the DMADV process as a critical tool for transitioning customer requirements into a product or process concept to be used in products under creation.

❑ **Six Sigma vs. kaizen.** Kaizen focuses on the continuous improvement of current processes. The Six Sigma DMAIC methodology is a rigorous form of kaizen. DMAIC also incorporates the ability to conduct a "kaizen blitz" after the Analyze step to capture early financial improvement gains.

❑ **Six Sigma vs. ISO 9000.** ISO 9000 is used to document the procedures used in a quality-management system. Six Sigma embeds results from improvement projects into the quality-management system. Thus, ISO 9000 is complementary to Six Sigma and is aligned with the business controls needed to ensure that performance gains are sustainable.

❑ **Six Sigma vs. statistical engineering.** The variables-search procedures used in statistical engineering have been incorporated into the Six Sigma DMAIC process with a richer use of statistical tools.

❑ **Six Sigma vs. DOE.** DOE is one of the most powerful tools in the Six Sigma toolkit. The procedures used in DOE are embedded throughout the Define, Measure, and Analyze steps of DMAIC, and DOE is the key methodology used in the Improve step.

❑ **Six Sigma vs. business-excellence assessment.** The various business-excellence assessment criteria provide business-focused methods for evaluating the performance of a business and identifying performance gaps that are opportunities for improvement. Six Sigma business leaders must generate Black Belt projects that are aligned with the organization's business strategy. Business-excellence self-assessment is an excellent contributor to this process.

❑ **Six Sigma vs. benchmarking.** Benchmarking was originally used as a stand-alone, operational tool to evaluate components of products and later used for the evaluation of business processes. Both applications are found in Six Sigma. Benchmarking for business-process performance is a key tool that helps business leaders use external comparisons to recognize performance gaps. Benchmarking can help teams to formulate new ideas and solutions during DMAIC or DMADV projects.

❑ **Six Sigma vs. BPR.** BPR was developed as a way to design new business processes using technology. DMADV can be regarded as a statistical approach to BPR when it is applied to business-process improvement rather than to new product or service development. Six Sigma is broader than BPR in that it does not rely on technology alone to make improvements; instead, it uses statistical tools to formulate the right process that incorporates the appropriate technology into the final solution. BPR fails to involve workers or gain their acceptance to proposed change, while Six Sigma builds collaboration among the implementing work force through their participation in the process design.

❑ **Six Sigma vs. the lean enterprise.** While the lean-enterprise approach focuses on improving the value stream of an organization by eliminating non-value-adding activities, Six Sigma improves an organization by increasing the consistency of its value-producing work. Lean tools are compatible with Green Belt programs because they do not require sophisticated mathematics or statistical software support. Many Six Sigma companies merge their Six Sigma and lean initiatives after recognizing the benefits of such integration.

Of the initiatives listed beforehand, only Six Sigma has been openly endorsed by leading executives in the business press. It has been evaluated by Wall Street stock analysts and found to provide a significant performance punch in many companies. It has also received the case-study attention of business schools around the world. General Electric used Six Sigma to grow their business after having implemented other change initiatives, and AlliedSignal (now Honeywell) used it to stimulate a successful organizational turnaround. During the 1990s, Six Sigma was used in more Fortune 500 organizations than any other improvement initiative, except for ISO 9000.

What does an executive sponsor do?

In the most successful Six Sigma initiatives, an organization's top business leaders serve as executive sponsors for the initiative's implementation and promote strategic alignment of Six Sigma projects. Strategic alignment means that the Six Sigma initiative concentrates on solving the most critical business problems while focusing continuous-improvement efforts on team-based projects. This way, management emphasizes continuous improvement while focusing breakthrough efforts on projects that will help achieve the organization's vision.

Top managers sponsoring a Six Sigma initiative focus on project selection and project management and fulfill the following roles:

- **Six Sigma program architect.** An organization's top leadership team establishes a framework for accomplishing their business objectives. Six Sigma acts as an initiative to stimulate action and coordinate activity to achieve these objectives.

- **Designer of strategic direction.** The executive sponsors of a Six Sigma initiative define the desired strategic direction of their business through the organizational structure and business systems that they implement. This direction is summarized in terms of the goals, objectives, and major change initiatives that the leadership team uses to enable the organization to move in a common direction.

- **Communicator of strategic direction.** Executive sponsors must be visible proponents of a Six Sigma initiative. They must initially describe and then frequently reinforce the organization's direction and rationale for their choices, and they must communicate progress made in achieving desired goals.

- **Cheerleader for Six Sigma efforts.** Management must encourage participants in Six Sigma projects by reminding them of the importance of their work. Such reminders range from an individual's initial invitation to become a Black Belt candidate to public recognition of excellence in accomplishing a Six Sigma project.

- **Reviewer of Six Sigma progress.** Top management must be responsible for ensuring that projects deliver the intended strategic direction. To do this, they must conduct high-level reviews of Six Sigma projects and request that the project champions or process owners conduct frequent, detailed reviews. These reviews are similar to the tollgate design reviews used by many R&D organizations.

- **Awarder of recognition.** Recognition is much more meaningful to employees when it comes with public ceremony and through the personal attention of respected business leaders. Executive sponsors must decide how they will recognize efforts and then be consistent about the way they implement this approach across the organization. Tying employee rewards and bonuses to the Six Sigma performance of their work areas is a good strategy.

❑ **Developer of guidelines and policy.** The executive sponsors of Six Sigma must be those leaders responsible for allocation of the organization's resources to achieve its business objectives. Top management must develop policies for implementation of Six Sigma in the areas listed below. Questions that must be answered in each area are also listed.

   – **Objectives for deployment of Six Sigma:** What challenge does the executive sponsor want to present to the organization? How will the challenge be measured? What is the timeline for achieving results?

   – **Requirements for management involvement in Six Sigma:** How should the organization's leaders be involved in Six Sigma? What is top management's expectation for their level of activity? Who will serve as deployment champion? Which managers will be the first project champions? How will this work be recognized?

   – **Black Belt selection criteria:** Which people should be chosen as candidates for Black Belt training? How can candidates be evaluated during the training to determine if they are likely to be successful?

   – **Training-project selection criteria:** What makes a good training project? What guidelines must be established for selection?

   – **Rules for determining Six Sigma financial benefits:** How will financial benefits be accrued for Six Sigma projects? What rules will be made to ensure that benefits from these projects are recognized properly and that they link to the organization's bottom-line results?

   – **System for recognition of Six Sigma results:** How will the various participants in the Six Sigma initiative be recognized and rewarded? This includes managers sponsoring Six Sigma projects, Black Belts conducting Six Sigma project analyses, individuals and team members working with the Black Belt on analysis or with the process owner on implementation, and the Master Black Belt, who serves as technical reviewer of the projects.

▶ **TIP**

Specific policies that top management should put in place at the beginning of a Six Sigma initiative include the following:

– Black Belts must be assigned to work on Six Sigma activities on a full-time basis. If Black Belts work on these projects on a part-time basis only, their effectiveness might be reduced.

– The organization's best high-potential people should be selected to become Black Belts. The Six Sigma methodology gives Black Belts the depth in thinking they need to drill down from strategic business issues to operational details. Completing Six Sigma projects gives Black Belts detailed knowledge of how business operations work.

- Projects chosen for Black Belt training must make a real business difference, hopefully within the scope of the current business plan. The organization will more readily accept Six Sigma if these projects are also challenging and the organization has not previously been able to tackle them with its customary way of working.

- Executive sponsors should personally charter projects and conduct executive-level reviews at initiation (charter approval), at the end of the DMA phase (to approve the pilot experiment), on completion of the Control step (to approve implementation), and on completion of the realization review (to ensure the projected bottom-line benefit has been attained).

Perhaps the most important aspect of the executive sponsor's job is the management of the Recognize step that precedes both DMAIC and DMADV. This task is conducted jointly by executive sponsors and business leaders. (The activities of the Recognize step are described in Question 8.)

While senior management sponsors Six Sigma, it usually designates one individual, typically the CEO, to serve as the spokesperson for Six Sigma implementation activities and communication. A deployment champion manages the logistics of implementation. (See Question 13 for more about the role of the deployment champion.)

QUESTION  5

Are you ready for Six Sigma?

How can you assess your organization's readiness for doing Six Sigma? How do you know that Six Sigma is the right next step to take? Such questions plague the beginning of any new initiative and must be resolved for management to have confidence in its decision.

Six Sigma changes an organization. Change, when directed by top management, is the result of a desire to move the organization in a particular direction. A change project is a set of actions taken to encourage organizational movement in that direction.

There are two aspects to any major change: the change required from the organization (i.e., the initiative or content of the change being made) and the change required from the organization's people (i.e., the personal transition to the new way of working). The initial reaction to a proposed change is typically resistance to shifting from a familiar way of working. Individual reactions vary from strong support to strong resistance, and executive sponsors of Six Sigma must understand the position of their business leaders so they can encourage them to embrace Six Sigma.

▶ TIP

It can be helpful to develop a matrix that uses a scale to judge the relative degree of acceptance of a Six Sigma initiative among an organization's leaders. Such a matrix, as outlined below, uses a five-point evaluation scheme that assesses their acceptance.

1. Highest level of support. A champion to make this work for the whole organization.

2. Moderate level of support. Proactive—willing to try a pilot project in his/her own area.

3. Neutral. Neither supporting nor resisting; taking a wait-and-see approach about changes.

4. Moderate level of resistance. ("My people are too busy with their real work.")

5. Strong level of resistance. ("Six Sigma will not work in our industry.")

Change-Initiative Acceptance Matrix

Business Leader	Strongly Against	Moderately Against	Neutral	Proactive	Champion
Person A		★—————	————→		
Person B			★———→		
Person C			★———	————→	
Person D				★———→	
Person E		★———→			
Person F				★———→	

Once the positions of an organization's leaders are identified, the executive sponsors can use this information to develop a strategy for getting the organization to embrace change.

To decide what change should be taken, managers often seek a respected competitor or a company in their industry that has implemented a change initiative and proven the methodology to be effective. They then use this organization as a case study to follow. However, this makes an organization a follower, rather than a leader, among its competitors.

What other options does management have? Perhaps the best is to conduct a self-assessment of the organization's readiness to adopt Six Sigma. Executives should also complete two other steps at the beginning of any major change process: designing the change initiative and applying the implementation strategy for business improvement. But before taking the steps to implement a change, consider the following areas of concern.

General change cautions

The most significant obstacles to successful change efforts exist in five areas of an organization: leadership, culture, communication, structure, and integration. Obstacles related to these five areas, and tips for addressing them, are described below.

Leadership can create major obstacles when its support diminishes over time due to a shift in interest to other management topics or to a new initiative. A Six Sigma program addresses this problem by encouraging active leadership involvement in project definition and review and in recognition of the efforts of Six Sigma professionals. Another area where leadership can create obstacles is the lack of involvement and support by middle management. In Six Sigma, this obstacle is addressed by having people at the middle-management level serving as project champions and process owners.

Cultural obstacles to change result from a fear of the unknown. These obstacles include resistance to change, skepticism, and an atmosphere of mistrust due to employees' fear of job loss. To alleviate concerns about job loss, management must convey to the organization the policy for work-force reductions that occur due to Six Sigma. Management must also seek ways to motivate and inspire employees to embrace Six Sigma as their normal way of working. In addition, management must ensure that high-potential employees don't miss promotional opportunities while working on Six Sigma projects. Using a proven change model as an outline for the organization's deployment plan is one way in which Six Sigma creates an atmosphere that encourages change.

Communication is a significant component of any change initiative. A lack of clear, coordinated communication across an organization can cause a change initiative to fail. By developing a specific communication plan to describe the organization's business strategy, goals, priorities, and expectations regarding Six Sigma, the deployment champion and steering committee can eliminate the uncertainty about change that comes from a lack of knowledge.

Structural obstacles to successful change include organizational structures that do not support the change initiative, budgetary limitations, and a lack of committed people to staff the initiative. A Six Sigma deployment plan addresses these issues to enable an entire organization to embrace Six Sigma.

The biggest integration obstacle to successful change is a lack of clear priority among the change initiatives management promotes. Six Sigma helps to eliminate this problem by encouraging executive sponsors to make key alignment decisions at the beginning of the implementation process and to communicate these decisions in their "elevator speech" about Six Sigma (see Question 1).

Problems can occur when change is not managed properly. Consider the following symptoms of poorly managed change initiatives:

❑ **Myopia:** A narrowness of vision that keeps management from seeing opportunities and threats from non-traditional sources.

❑ **Not invented here:** The feeling that nothing has merit for an organization unless it was first invented or developed within the organization.

❑ **Unintended consequences:** Getting something that you didn't want instead of the result for which you planned.

❑ **Confusion:** The lack of clarity that occurs when different parts of an organization have a different understanding of the direction in which senior management wants to go.

❑ **Internal competition:** A focus on competition among internal business units that averts the organization's focus away from its customers and external competitors.

❑ **Repetition of mistakes:** Making the same mistakes that were made during a prior change initiative. This symptom typically occurs when the management team does not explore potential improvement opportunities from previous initiatives or do a post-mortem analysis to find out what went well.

❑ **Resistance to change:** A general symptom of an ineffective change initiative, this typically indicates that one or more core concerns have not been properly addressed in the change-management planning.

- ❑ **Gamesmanship:** This occurs when managers believe they can alter the way a change initiative operates to make it suit their need not to change. Whenever managers re-create elements of a change initiative, they create a local standard that is no longer part of the organization-wide initiative.

- ❑ **False start:** This occurs when an initiative begins in part of an organization without the support of the top management team. The initiative must then be restarted with the full support and active engagement of the senior management team.

- ❑ **Settling:** The point at which an organization, unable to replicate the success achieved at other organizations, decides to accept a lesser level of success by declaring victory even though it has not achieved its initial goals.

Six Sigma–specific change cautions

Below is a list of some specific problems that can occur with a Six Sigma implementation. An organization must include appropriate countermeasures for these problems in its Six Sigma deployment planning.

- ❯ Misalignment with the organization's culture.
- ❯ Failure to convince leadership of the value of Six Sigma.
- ❯ Lack of management involvement.
- ❯ Black Belt candidates who are not capable of performing the analyses or providing training to others.
- ❯ Poor selection of Black Belt training projects.
- ❯ Projects that are too broad, too narrow, or ill-defined.
- ❯ Insufficient communication of success stories.
- ❯ Unavailability of Master Black Belt coaches.
- ❯ Little integration with the balanced-scorecard measurement system or business strategy.
- ❯ Low priority for Six Sigma improvements.
- ❯ Inadequate resources allocated to implementation of projects or to support management of the Six Sigma initiative.

Conducting a change-readiness assessment

Performing a change-readiness assessment will enable you to determine whether a Six Sigma initiative is right for your organization and whether your organization is ready for this type of change. Consider the following four readiness factors for Six Sigma.

1. The degree to which change initiatives have been successfully incorporated in the past and why. Reviewing these past efforts can often enlighten the top management team about what it must do to improve the organization's ability to accept such changes in the future.

2. An organization's ability to define project scope realistically. Many organizations tend to define projects with such a broad scope that they become almost impossible to achieve. Organizations with a successful rate of project completion know how to define the scope of projects in a way that makes them easier to complete. The number of projects completed drives the return an organization achieves on its Six Sigma investment; the more projects completed, the higher the return.

3. The management team's constancy of purpose in its strategic direction. Does Six Sigma align to the organization's long-term strategic direction? Has this direction persisted long enough that employees believe all efforts tied to it have the full attention of the top management team? Whenever possible, Six Sigma should be integrated with the organization's main concerns and interpreted as an implementation toolkit for its strategic projects.

4. An organization's approach toward employee development. Many organizations have difficulty finding challenging jobs to keep their high-potential employees productively engaged in activities that broaden their knowledge of the organization and its business. Six Sigma provides this opportunity by creating positions for Black Belts and Master Black Belts. The knowledge that these people gain enhances their careers and prepares them for cross functional positions where they can further develop their business knowledge.

▶ TIP

When evaluating your organization's readiness to accept a Six Sigma change initiative, consider its strength in the following areas. Incorporating these business-improvement factors into a change-management initiative helps to ensure broader acceptance of a desired change, a smoother transition, and accelerated implementation.

- Propensity to adapt and experiment. How willing is the organization to change the way it works, either in incremental steps or with major initiatives? Are managers open to experimentation with process improvements to see what works best?

- Degree of success with the last major change. How much success was achieved with the last major change initiative? Did it meet its objectives? Did you learn from the success or failure of this initiative?

- Access to information and resources. Is information needed to plan or implement new work processes readily accessible to those who need it? Are enough resources allocated to ensure that management's priority projects and initiatives are effectively implemented?

- Management tolerance for delays and failures. Does management realize experiments can lead to success or failure and that their main purpose is to gain profound knowledge? Do management personnel tolerate delays in programs in an effort to get them right, or do they force a solution with unproven or unknown consequences just to keep on schedule?

- Level of interpersonal trust. How much trust do employees have in the motives of the management team? Do employees believe top management personnel are credible and that they communicate truthfully about the rationale for the desired change?

- Comfort level with change. How comfortable is the organization with change? Do employees accept it without question, or is there significant resistance to all change initiatives? Is this attitude consistent across all layers of the organization?

- Willingness to cooperate. What is the degree of employee willingness to take an active role in change initiatives to ensure that change is achieved in a timely and effective manner?

- Management commitment. How strongly does the top management team feel about the desired change? Will the senior leaders commit to the initiative as a new way of working?

- Leadership capability of teams. Do the teams in the organization's various business units have a solid leadership capability? Will Black Belts challenge the leadership of the local process owners, or will they perceive these people as peers?

- Culture of continuous improvement. Does the organization have a strong culture of continuous improvement, or is it more focused on controlling all work to maintain process performance? Do people believe that it is their responsibility to continuously improve the quality of their work output?

- Delegation of decision authority. Has decision authority been delegated to the level where process-performance knowledge allows the best decisions to be made, or are such decisions closely held by senior business leaders?

- Approach to standardization. Does the organization accept work standards as the best way to ensure consistency in performance across shifts and work units, or do individual business units seek to develop their own work procedures for common activities?

Use a scale like the one on the next page to indicate your organization's degree of conformity to these performance factors.

Change-Readiness Assessment

Criterion	Low 1	2	Neutral 3	4	High 5	SCORE
Propensity to adapt and experiment						
Degree of success with last major change						
Access to information and resources						
Management tolerance for delay and failure						
Level of interpersonal trust						
Comfort level with change						
Willingness to cooperate						
Management will for achieving new state						
Leadership capability of local process teams						
Culture of continuous improvement						
Degree of delegation of decision authority						
Acceptability of work standardization						
Business need for Six Sigma						
Time available to pursue strategic change						
					Total	

When a readiness assessment indicates your organization is not ready for implementing Six Sigma, you should develop and implement a change-management process that will make the organization ready for successful change. This can be accomplished during the pilot phase of your Six Sigma program. By following a change model, you can ensure that all the appropriate steps are taken for a successful change, emphasizing the areas where management believes there is a need for improvement.

▶ TIP

If your leadership team is unsure how Six Sigma applies to your business, conduct a pilot experiment by applying it to one small part of the business that represents a major business focus area.

How do I do it?

Try the following steps to perform a self-assessment of your organization's readiness to implement a Six Sigma business-improvement initiative.

1. Customize the criteria for the readiness assessment and the scale to be used in making the self-assessment.

2. Develop a standard procedure for conducting a self-assessment.

3. Train leaders of different parts of your organization in the procedure for leading a self-assessment.

4. Conduct intact management team self-assessments using the self-assessment process.

5. Consolidate the results from all parts of your organization in a way that identifies those areas that are most prepared for a Six Sigma implementation.

6. Identify those areas where your organization is neutral or below specific counter-measures and include this information in your deployment plan to ensure overall success of your change-implementation efforts.

Designing the change initiative

Once management decides on the need to change and determines its strategic direction, then it must create a plan that the organization can use to make the change happen. Planning the deployment of a change requires the participation of the full management team to create support for the initiative. This ensures that the plan includes all the core elements required for the change to be successful. It is important to have consistency across the entire organization for implementing all major changes that modify the framework or architecture of your business processes.

▶ TIP

Change must be managed at both the organization (macro) level and the individual-project (micro) level. The following model for macro-level change is a ready-to-adapt framework for introducing planned changes to an organization's strategic work.

1. Creating a shared need. Management must determine how much change is required and where it is needed, and then it must structure a business case to change. For a change to succeed, the need to change must be greater than the resistance to it. What reason is compelling enough for the entire organization to accept it as the need to make the proposed change?

2. Shaping a common vision. The vision of the organization after the desired change occurs must be acceptable to the entire organization. One way to shape a common vision is to involve all employees in a strategic dialogue (see the next page) about the business case for change.

3. Mobilizing universal involvement. Management must find ways to involve as many individuals as possible in the change initiative. Attempts to change the organization won't last unless they are supported by its formal structures; business processes; measurement, appraisal, and reward systems; staffing practices; and design of its core work processes. Six Sigma improvement projects should involve every employee.

4. Accelerating the transition. Fast change and lasting change are two very different things. Fast change can be made by using pilot demonstration projects to illustrate the value of change. Lasting change must incorporate all formal management systems. To accelerate a lasting transition, a detailed deployment plan must be created to guide and coordinate all improvement activities.

5. Monitoring implementation progress. To sustain momentum and keep the change happening, an organization must continuously perceive that the change initiative has the attention and full support of the top management team. Senior management must review operating measures for deployment of the Six Sigma program, assess progress reports on projects of high management interest, and conduct periodic audits of the Six Sigma implementation.

Strategic dialogue

Strategic dialogue is a process that engages members of the organization in an open discussion about the business case for change. It gives all employees access to key data regarding the formulation of the business strategy and allows them to express their ideas about actions the company should take. Such a discussion is a major source of strategic business-improvement ideas for Six Sigma projects.

A strategic dialogue goes through a three-phase process: opening, sorting, and closing. Consider the following plan for conducting a strategic dialogue.

OPENING: Discovering the options for change

1. Formulate the business case for change. Describe why the change needs to be made to the organization in terms of financial returns. What steps must the organization take to improve its business performance? Why is this a priority for the organization?

2. Conduct an external study of organizations in similar circumstances. Search to find other organizations that have had similar circumstances and benchmark what they did to improve. What were their results? How applicable is their situation to your organization?

3. Convene a senior management workshop. Use this meeting to prepare the initial round of the strategic dialogue. What are the critical assumptions about the business that must be challenged? How will today's business change as a result of external forces? Which forces are the most critical given the organization's intellectual capital, product portfolio, and competitive environment? Which technologies are most likely to change the way the market accepts your products? What intellectual property does your organization own that can make a difference in this future environment?

4. Develop "white papers" to summarize the initial dialogue. Prepare white papers that define the challenge to your organization's critical business assumptions, business model, or product portfolio. Each white paper must also describe the challenge's impact on the business case and identify questions that must be answered to determine the priority of the challenge and to shape a strategy that responds to it.

5. Assign a business leader to champion each white paper. Each white paper should be assigned to a business leader who will direct the strategic dialogue and act as an advocate for this issue during the closing sessions of the strategic dialogue.

6. Publish the white papers on the organization's intranet. Make each white paper the topic of a chat room. A business leader (or an assistant) moderates each chat room and keeps the dialogue on topic.

7. Solicit chat-room dialogue about each white paper. Publish the chat-room address for each white paper and ask employees to input their ideas about the topic and the challenges the organization faces. By participating in the dialogue, employees become more aware of the strategic issues confronting the organization and better understand the business.

CLOSING: Making choices of desired path

8. Consolidate the discussions from the chat rooms. Use an Affinity Diagram to determine interrelationships among the ideas presented in the chat rooms. What does the data say about the issue? What ideas do people have about making improvements in this area? What breakthrough concepts have been identified as worthy to pursue for more detailed investigation?

9. Incorporate chat-room input into the organization's strategic plan. As the strategic plan is formally constructed, use the data from the consolidated chat-room input to stimulate ideas about opportunities to improve the business. A problem presented in one of these dialogues might be an opportunity to grow the business in an exceptional way.

10. Present the results of the strategic dialogue. Publish the resulting plan and final strategic-dialogue findings on the intranet for employees to study. This enables you to build more-effective implementation plans that are closely aligned with the chosen strategic direction.

In the opening phase of a strategic dialogue, the job is to generate alternatives so the number of options grows significantly. In the sorting phase, the task is to structure these options before making a decision. Duplications are eliminated, and alternatives are combined. In the closing phase, the work focuses on finding the best option. This can be represented graphically as follows:

Three Phases of a Strategic Dialogue

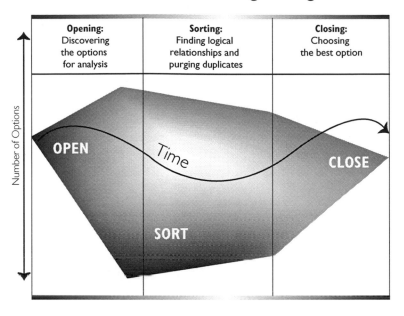

Opening: Discovering the options for analysis	Sorting: Finding logical relationships and purging duplicates	Closing: Choosing the best option

What are the basic requirements for people to be successful in their work? Consider a model for work that includes the following elements:

A Success Model for Work

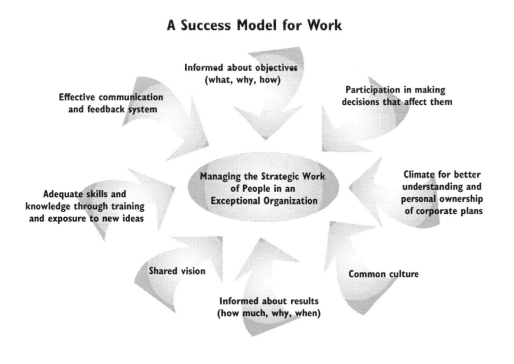

Note that these are the same elements that are essential to manage change effectively. The key to making change management work is a thorough implementation of the plan: All questions have been anticipated, and recommendations based on a sound data analysis are presented as alternatives for making improvements.

Implementation management

Deploying an implementation plan is perhaps the most difficult aspect of any change-management effort because it engages the human dimension of the organization. This is the "soft" aspect of management—leadership of people rather than management by the numbers. Implementation follows a detailed model at the project level for each change that is made, as illustrated below.

Effective Implementation of Change

Process Steps / Supporting Actions	Diagnose	Design	Develop	Decide	Deploy
Create a shared vision and mutual respect by values.	What are the critical business issues over the coming strategic-planning horizon?	Generate a vision that is compatible with the strategic direction.	How does vision fit with history, values, culture, management style, and stakeholder concerns?	Clarify options and select what is best by senior management consensus.	Tell the story to all stakeholders. Build commitment buy-in from all constituents.
Demonstrate top management commitment to vision and values.	How will people know that the managers are committed?	Develop a plan to demonstrate the commitment of the top managers.	How feasible are the alternatives? Is the achievement of the vision believable?	What are the best alternatives? Are decision criteria commonsense?	Agree on the key behavioral styles needed to manage and assign people to critical positions.
Staff projects with the right people and skills.	How well do the current staffing and skill structure support the vision?	What alternatives are there for narrowing the gap?	Check each option for feasibility, degree of change, chance for success, and cost.	Based on this analysis, select the best option.	Hand off to the rest of the organization; set goals and deploy throughout all levels.
Set the measures, targets, feedback, and rewards to support learning and behavior.	What is currently being measured? What feedback and rewards are used today?	Generate options: * What to measure * How to give feedback * What to reward * How to reward	Evaluate options for effectiveness. Pilot options in small units or teams to validate.	Decide which of these options best reinforces the desired behaviors.	Roll out the measurement, feedback, and reward systems together.
Communicate clearly and regularly to build interest in change projects.	What are the processes for management communication? Consider both the informal and formal.	What new ways to communicate can be developed? Is communication upward effective?	How will each communication option support the operating style of managers? Is it effective?	Decide on the best means to enhance total communication.	Implement the communication tactics and new dialogue vehicles.

Following the five-step Diagnose-Design-Develop-Decide-Deploy process shown in the figure above at the project level ensures that the detail of the change initiative is structured in a way that the organization will readily accept. When an organization's strategic work—that which is required to conduct the primary business of the organization—is changed, it is important for management to align its resources and infrastructure to make the change happen.

Overcoming fear and inertia

Sometimes, despite the best planning, people still resist making a change. The five main reasons why some people and organizations resist implementing Six Sigma are as follows:

1. Fear of statistics. This can occur with Black Belt candidates and process owners, who must be able to read and interpret the results of statistical analyses.

2. Increased uncertainty when cutting costs. Cost-cutting brings into question the continuity of an organization and its ability to survive.

3. Inertia from the "same old way" of doing things. It is hard to do things differently when the old way of working is habitual.

4. An attitude that improvement is not possible. An organization can become overly comfortable with its past successes. To avoid this, during good times management personnel should say they are pleased that returns are sufficient, but they recognize opportunities exist to do even better. This instills greater expectations for the future within the organization.

5. Insecurity and angst. These conditions exist in most organizations faced with a potential for downsizing. When employees' security or safety needs are threatened, their attention shifts away from the higher principles that support continuous improvement of the organization.

How does an organization overcome fear and inertia to make a change? Here are some recommendations:

▶ The organization's top executive must act as the driving force behind the implementation of Six Sigma methods, encouraging the accompanying cultural change to management by fact, accountability, empowered decision-making, and cross-functional teamwork to accomplish shared business objectives.

▶ A senior manager who directly reports to the top management team should be named the organization's deployment champion. This person will oversee and coordinate the Six Sigma initiative across the entire organization.

▶ The organization should establish a recruiting and selection process in its infrastructure to ensure that its best and brightest become Black Belts—the "analytical engines" who drive the change process one project at a time.

▶ Embedding the following list of core principles into your Six Sigma initiative can help to make it stronger. The greater the presence of these dimensions in a change initiative, the greater the probability of achieving sustained performance improvement.

NOTE

Business leaders must be prepared for resistance to change during the early stages of Six Sigma deployment. Identifying sources of potential resistance and developing a strategy to deal with resistance are key enablers of a smooth implementation.

Core principles of change

▶ Information must be used for improvement, not to judge or control people.

▶ Authority must be equal to responsibility.

▶ There must be rewards for results.

▶ Cooperation must be the basis for working together.

▶ Employees must feel secure in their employment. Their job might change, but they must not feel that their livelihood is threatened.

▶ Employees should have an ownership stake.

▶ There must be a climate of fairness:

  – Compensation should be equitable and set objectively, not subjectively.

  – Make sure people are given equivalent rewards for similar performance. Avoid any actual or apparent special treatment of favorite employees who have not earned award or recognition.

  – Give employees meaningful influence over decisions about their own work, with a special emphasis on accomplishing work goals and solving problems.

  – Adhere to clear standards that are seen as just and reasonable. Do not give praise that is out of proportion to accomplishments or impose a penalty disproportionate to an offense.

  – Demonstrate respect toward employees and recognize their strengths and contributions.

  – Follow due process. Make sure all procedures are open to public scrutiny, and permit everyone to participate actively in their application.

▶ TIP

Three conditions must be met for management to be able to properly hold individuals accountable for the quality of their work. These conditions must be met in the following sequence to be effective:

1. People must have *capability*: knowledge of the job they are asked to do. They must also be trained in the methods required to do it effectively.

2. People must have *responsibility*: knowledge of the standard of performance they are asked to attain. An objective measurement system must be in place to evaluate their performance.

3. People must have *authority*: the ability to self-regulate their own work. They must be able to observe the work-process measures and make decisions about corrective actions so they can keep their process operating according to the standard.

How can Six Sigma change a company's culture?

The following cultural changes are likely to result in an organization from a successful Six Sigma implementation:

❏ The organization develops an intolerance for variation in process performance and results. Employees seek to deliver consistent output to customers, and they use innovation to create the next generation of business processes and products.

❏ Assigned managers "own" specific processes, ensuring performance and coordination of improvement activities.

❏ Instead of focusing on traditional financial results, the organization monitors process-performance measures to ensure the desired financial outcomes are achieved.

❏ Senior managers hold process owners accountable for performance that measures up to the targets.

❏ Solutions to business problems create sustainable gains rather than requiring subsequent projects to fix processes that drift away from their target performance.

❏ Customers are satisfied with the consistency of performance. This results in customer loyalty.

❏ Organization-wide learning ensures rapid implementation of best practices.

❏ Collaboration exists among all supply-chain partners, both internal and external—including customers.

❏ In all communications, members of the organization use data to support their opinions.

These changes combine to make a deep and substantial shift in the way an organization is managed. Business leaders must anticipate this shift in management style and encourage the organization to move in the desired direction. They must also anticipate any barriers to change that are likely to occur in their organization and work to eliminate them.

Why use a martial-arts analogy?

The names originally chosen for Six Sigma specialists use an analogy from karate. In this form of martial arts, each pupil continuously improves, mastering ever-more-difficult methods and demonstrating achievement through real-world competition. Recognition for their demonstrated progress is a colored sash, or "belt," that demonstrates mastery. But this achievement is not the end of the journey. Continuous development of Black Belts occurs as they master higher-level methods and progress through nine levels of advanced performance.

The original rationale for this martial-arts analogy was that Six Sigma focuses on personal achievement (progression through the various levels of recognition) and competition (head-to-head marketing). Many companies today find that the original rationale does not serve their business needs. But this should not prevent them from implementing the principles, methods, and techniques of Six Sigma. Selecting other names for Six Sigma specialists enables an organization to avoid problems from using a martial-arts analogy that does not work in their culture.

▶ TIP

Although the original Black Belt nomenclature may not fit your organization's internal needs, attaining the level of recognition that this title represents is an important professional achievement. On your organization's certificates of recognition, it's a good idea to say that the recipient "has completed a four-week program of study in the Black Belt body of Six Sigma knowledge and the required project work." This can help to assure your customers that your Black Belt–level Six Sigma specialists have followed the recognized approach to training and not merely taken a course of lesser proportion that does not measure up to the standard meaning of this job title.

What is strategic about Six Sigma?

For an organization to maximize business benefits, it should incorporate Six Sigma in its strategic planning and implementation processes. It is the principal responsibility of management to establish the business context for an organization's Six Sigma improvement efforts. By choosing projects that improve an organization's high-priority work processes—those that contribute most to its business performance—management can ensure significant gains from a Six Sigma initiative.

Six Sigma is a strategic intervention, not a business strategy. If business leaders make the wrong choices regarding products, services, or technologies, then Six Sigma can facilitate doing the wrong things well. Part of the obligation of business leaders is to set the right direction for product- or service-line choices.

Six Sigma as a Management Process

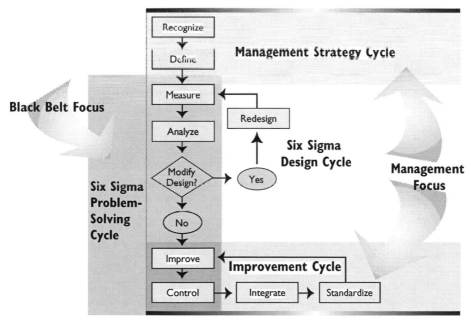

To achieve this focus, management personnel must first determine their priority business-improvement needs. This preliminary step, which precedes all Six Sigma projects, is called the Recognize step. During this step, management conducts a current-state analysis of the business. This involves diagnosing current and prospective business vulnerabilities, determining the organization's best technologies and product innovations and their potential sales, determining the adequacy of the current strategic intent, and allocating resources to achieve the organization's objectives for short-term profit and long-term strength.

Once such an analysis is completed, leaders then decide the best direction to take. Strategic choice and follow-up action are the objectives of business measurement and strategic planning. Excellence comes from execution, not from the mere effort of business analysis.

A sound practice is to choose Six Sigma projects that implement an organization's most important strategies. By identifying the direction in which the organization needs to move and breaking down this plan into manageable projects, business leaders focus their Six Sigma resources on driving strategic change. They prioritize among the projects from a business perspective. Below are some tips for identifying strategic-change projects and then deploying them as Six Sigma Black Belt projects.

❏ Six Sigma begins with discovering what customers really want—not just assuming the organization understands its customer requirements or just providing what it has available to deliver to customers. Six Sigma starts with the customer and dives deeply into the work processes that deliver customer value to determine the source of problems.

❏ Six Sigma projects use a specific elimination sequence to solve problems. They first eliminate variety, then non-value-added work, and then variance within a work process. Six Sigma seeks to eliminate a problem rather than trying to find a set of conditions that controls its occurrence.

❏ Managers apply Six Sigma one project at a time. As a general rule, they should initiate projects that have the highest potential for contributing to profitable performance and increasing customer satisfaction.

❏ The process-optimization phase of a Six Sigma project normally takes from one to two months, depending on data availability or the ability to conduct a designed experiment. Benefits are seen within a month of project completion, depending on how aggressively the process owner implements the recommendations.

❏ The Six Sigma analysis process enables an organization to learn about the way its work is done. Each step in the analysis process should lead to new knowledge about what is important for the long-term success of a work process. The analysis process's rigorous investigation steps and fixed sequence of probing questions lead to profound knowledge about the root cause(s) of problems and help identify opportunities for improvement. To learn about a work process, it is necessary to get data about its performance. The following questions will help uncover what is most important about a work process's operation:

    1. What do you want to know?

2. How do you want to graphically display what you need to know?

3. What tool will generate what you need to see?

4. What type of data is required to use this tool?

5. Where can you get this type of data?

6. How much of this data will you need?

7. How will a random sampling of data be ensured?

The Recognize step

The Recognize step is the structured process that managers use to identify potential projects for Black Belts to solve. It precedes the DMAIC process and provides the direction for DMADV improvement efforts.

The objective of this step is to identify the business focus for Six Sigma projects. This step ensures that improvements made to a process will make a strategic difference to the organization. This step also forces the management team to choose one of several competing problem areas for the use of capital budgets. By looking at its internal operations, the organization should be able to see the areas of greatest opportunity for business improvement.

During this step, top management localizes a high-priority business problem to the areas of the organization that it affects. Management might name an executive sponsor for the problem to lead the effort to improve performance. A management team can be formed to compile the background information required to launch a Black Belt project.

The Recognize step involves several efforts:

❑ Customer and market analysis to determine critical areas for business focus

❑ Current-state analysis to evaluate gaps in performance-management systems and to align the organization with its strategic direction

❑ Using measurement systems that monitor performance and determine the root cause of problems

❑ Prioritization of resources for the organization's most important objectives

What business leaders must do during the Recognize step

❑ Identify areas where improvement is most needed for the organization to achieve competitive performance.

❑ Link the focus of the Six Sigma initiative to the areas of most vital customer significance.

❑ Choose the right people to serve as project champions and Black Belts.

- Identify projects that are achievable and that will prove the superiority of Six Sigma methods over previous improvement attempts in the organization.

Fundamental questions to ask during the Recognize step

- How well are we performing relative to our competition?
- What are business metrics, and how are measurement criteria established for each metric?
- Do our business metrics link to our competitive criteria?
- If so, how do we choose where to make improvements?
- If not, what must we change?
- How often should business metrics be recorded and reviewed?
- How accurate are our business metrics? Does the way we illustrate them in graphs and charts allow us to interpret them correctly?
- How do we prioritize among competing alternatives?
- What are the critical assumptions in our business model? Are any processes creating a business bottleneck?
- What is the cost of poor quality in these processes?
    - Which of these processes are most strategic?
    - Do any of these processes influence our critical business assumptions?
- Which processes are most visible to external customers?
- What criteria should we emphasize when defining Six Sigma projects?

Deliverables of the Recognize step

- A prioritized portfolio of potential Six Sigma projects that are aligned with the strategic intent and long-term direction of the organization.
- Prioritization of projects for best resource utilization.
- Identification of business objectives.
- Definition of business metrics.
- Definition of the value proposition for key stakeholders.
- Recognition of problem areas.
- Sponsorship of corrective action.
- Strategic alignment.
- Project-selection criteria.
- Prioritization of projects into a portfolio for analysis.

- Decisions for capital budget regarding projects.
- Establishment of executive sponsorship for oversight.
- Identification of business leaders to champion the project(s).
- Identification of process owners to help with project definition.
- Assignment of Master Black Belt(s) and Black Belt(s) to conduct the study.

Techniques that support analysis in the Recognize step

- Business enterprise model
- Business measurement map
- Balanced scorecard report
- Strategic-planning process
- Competitive-industry studies
- Business-excellence self-assessment
- Critical business assumptions
- Business scenario analysis
- Vulnerability analysis (strengths, weaknesses, opportunities, and threats, or SWOT)

Can Six Sigma include business excellence?

Business excellence is the simultaneous delivery of value to three types of stakeholders: financial (owners and investors), commercial (markets and customers), and social (employees and society). Business excellence is achieved through conducting a self-assessment against business-improvement criteria based on best practices at leading companies and then acting to close gaps in performance based on this self-assessment.

The principal focus of a Six Sigma–based management system is to reduce variation in business and work processes. This creates a predictable business in which work processes are designed to deliver expected results. This approach requires business managers to (1) know the variation inherent in the business and the resulting implications for managing work processes and (2) focus the entire organization on its strategic objectives. When a business routinely delivers expected performance outcomes and knows the contribution of its work processes to this overall result, management has done its job.

How Six Sigma relates to business-excellence programs

Business excellence is the result of the effective satisfaction of both (1) and (2) above. One key to achieving performance excellence is proper design and execution of the organization's measurement system. This is a core feature of the business-excellence approach of both the Baldrige Award and the European Quality Award. In these business-improvement schemes, the primary jobs of leaders are to establish direction, ensure that good measurements are taken, review performance, and make choices that result in the achievement of desired business goals. The Six Sigma approach to management provides the analytic discipline to achieve the performance these business-excellence models require.

Six Sigma blends an organization's need for good leadership with its need for good management. Good leadership encourages an organization to either take a direction it has not previously taken or to maintain a constancy in purpose by acting strategically. Good management, on the other hand, encourages an organization to perform consistently and conduct its routine tasks efficiently and economically so it delivers its customers' performance expectations. Consistent performance results when an organization's coordinated work activities are predictable outcomes that occur because of the way the work is designed.

Performance-measurement systems found in business-excellence models measure work processes in a way that cumulatively predicts the overall outcome of the organization's efforts to deliver customer expectations. Local measures are valid statistical predictors of the global business performance. Thus, the system is designed logically to ensure that operational actions are properly reflected in strategic outcomes. Performance excellence is an intentional act of leadership.

Performance-excellence models have two distinct indicators of successful results: the confidence customers have in their relationship with the business and the confidence that investors place in the business for continued profitable growth.

What is the purpose of a business?

The purpose of a business is to make a profit for its owners by delivering value to its customers. A business must serve its customers, or it will not be sustainable over time. On the journey to achieve this goal, several supporting goals must be achieved:

❑ Customers must be satisfied.

❑ Financial assets must be prudently managed.

❑ Sound working practices must be developed.

❑ Employees must be motivated to contribute their best efforts.

The principal source of external funds to satisfy an organization's financial needs is its customers. Without continuing purchases by customers, there is no return on an owner's invested capital. Thus, a strong focus on satisfying the customer is a significant ingredient in any company's recipe for sustained success. Continued growth and profitability are necessary to overcome inflation and obsolescence due to new technology or emerging markets. If these goals are not met, then the best quality system in the world will not sustain an organization's performance. It will die from lack of customers.

Savvy leaders know what business actions are required to consistently produce outcomes that are desired by an organization's stakeholders. This is the key to sustainable success. They know what actions to take by using a well-designed measurement system that culminates in a customer dashboard for these critical business issues. The first step toward designing such a system is to understand the standards for success and how they work.

Enduring standards for business success

The only enduring standards for business success are the long-term performance indicators of its two external focus areas: customers and shareholders. Typically the success of a business is measured in financial terms, such as operating profit, return on net assets, earnings per share, return on capital, return on investment, and cash flow. These measures indicate the ability of a company to deliver financial value to customers and shareholders alike.

But financial results are *lagging indicators*; they provide only a backward look at business performance and give no hint of a company's future performance. Good top-tier measurement systems must indicate performance in both financial and market dimensions while also providing diagnostic measures that indicate where performance problems exist and why. They must also be capable of predicting changes in an organization's financial performance based on observations of changes in its work processes. That is, they are *leading indicators*, which can be used to predict future results from the actions of today.

The following list describes conditions that often demonstrate that a business is delivering short-term financial success and providing a credible promise of long-term commercial strength.

❑ Gross revenue increases faster than the cost of operations (when revenue growth is stimulated by innovation rather than acquisition).

❑ Sales-transaction volume increases and transaction cost decreases.

❑ New products have better quality (i.e., fewer defects or customer complaints) than the ones they replace.

❑ Capital payback periods are consistently reduced.

❑ Product warranty claims, product returns, customer complaints, labor-cost variance, scrap, and rework all decrease simultaneously.

❑ There are consistent and sustained trends in satisfaction improvement for targeted customers.

❑ Sales growth is continuous across product generations.

❑ Opportunities for innovation are abundant, and emerging technologies are rapidly introduced as successful new products.

Many of these performance indicators are related to "business X's"; that is, they measure specific performance that can be related to either DMAIC or DMADV projects. Six Sigma measurement systems must satisfy two key criteria: (1) they must indicate success against the objectives of the business, and (2) they must provide diagnostic support by decomposing the $y = f(x)$ analysis when top-tier indicators show there is something wrong. Creating a Six Sigma measurement system begins by establishing these top-tier metrics and then decomposing the measurement system according to the MECE logic of $y = f(x)$. (See Question 12 for details on this process.)

One principal metric for evaluating business performance is shareholder value-added, or SVA (see Question 10). The second is related to the value-added for customers—sometimes called market value-added (MVA) or brand value-added (BVA). (See Question 11.) Financial and customer value are linked together in the Recognize step of Six Sigma when management's actions on behalf of the customers drive the financial return for shareholders. In the language of Six Sigma, these key result areas of a business that indicate success to its most important stakeholders are called the "business Y's" of an organization. All organizations tend to evaluate themselves using two key performance areas for their business Y's: financial performance and market performance.

QUESTION 10

How can Six Sigma improve financial value?

An organization's financial success is typically measured from the shareholder's perspective by the value added to the initial shareholder investment. This is called shareholder value-added (SVA). SVA reflects financial-performance results and takes into account three primary factors: cash, return, and growth. These are explained below.

❑ **Cash:** The two aspects of this factor are the generation of enough cash to fund operations and the way cash is used. The tool used for evaluating performance is *cash-flow analysis*, an indicator of the flow of income compared to the expenses the income must cover. Cash-flow analysis also evaluates the timing of an organization's finances.

❑ **Return:** This is the profit (i.e., return on assets, capital, or investment) that a business makes based on its operations. Return has two key ingredients: profit margin and velocity. The profit margin is the surplus generated over expenses. The velocity is the speed at which revenue is generated from sales to customers. The basic management rule for business return is that it must be greater than the "cost of capital" (i.e., the profit returned from an investment is greater than the interest of a bank loan).

❑ **Growth:** If growth is not profitable, then the organization's ability to sustain the way it operates is limited and the business will not generate the return required to realize its strategic growth objective.

Interpreting SVA is easy: If it is positive, investor value is being created, relative to investments with similar opportunities for returns. If it is negative, investor value is being destroyed. SVA links internal financial performance and external objectives, evaluates the use of net income by determining if asset levels are too high for the revenue they generate, tracks whether shareholder value is being increased or destroyed, and demonstrates if business growth is profitable. These factors clearly indicate an organization's financial picture.

Determining process capability

Shareholder value, which is an external measurement, is not the only way to evaluate an organization's financial performance. A helpful internal measurement—known as Return on Capital Employed (ROCE)—determines the return on capital after it has been invested by the shareholder. This performance metric is particularly good for indicating the performance of a resource-intensive business.

A business that is capital-intensive monitors its ROCE to determine whether management is being a good steward of investors' funds. If the capital is well employed, the return on investment should also be evident in the organization's work process. Too often, management personnel base their judgments about performance not on data-based analysis, but on what they think is happening based on subjective observations. ROCE can be used for the top-tier financial metrics in a Six Sigma measurement system. (For more information on Six Sigma business-measurement systems, see Question 44.)

Two factors that can help build understanding about the efficiency of daily operations are customer requirements and *process variation*, the natural variation that a process exhibits over time. Dividing the process variation (six standard deviations' worth) into the designed customer requirements results in a value known as *process capability (Cp)*. This level of performance represents the outcome that management and customers can reasonably expect.

A second ratio used to judge the performance of a work process is Cpk, which represents a process's variation in performance from its average performance to the closest specification limit. A process with an observed Cpk of 1.5 or higher is performing at six sigma relative to the customers' requirements. As long as a process operates in a stable manner and is not affected by any special causes of variation, it will reliably deliver customers' expectations.

The gap between Cp and Cpk represents an opportunity for improvement from an under-performing work process. Closing this gap will improve process performance by centering the process with respect to its specification. This reduces the potential for poor quality and maximizes the ROCE for the capital equipment that is used.

How can Six Sigma improve customer value?

An organization attains customer value by consistently providing its customers with goods or services that meet their needs. Customer value cannot be accurately measured with customer-satisfaction forms because they are often biased by a customer's latest experience. A better way to measure customer value is to evaluate the accumulated effect of satisfaction over the long term using *brand value*. This is based on an organization's projected future revenue potential, which is determined by the sustained level of customer satisfaction and the organization's ability to ensure a sustainable or growing market share.

Brand value is built one customer at a time. By providing customers with confidence that their voices will be heard and their needs will be met, an organization creates loyal customers who believe the company stands for enduring value. A brand merits long-term appreciation when it is dedicated to consistently delivering a strong customer-centric value proposition regardless of changes in technology or competitors. Brand value gives customers confidence that over the long term the company will always meet their needs.

Brand value–added (BVA) is the premium price that one brand demands over its competition because of its higher merits relative to its competitors and market expectations of its future performance. These expectations are conditioned by the way a company has serviced its customers in the past. BVA differs from market value-added (MVA), which is the value added to a share price beyond the book value of a stock.

BVA is estimated using three components: (1) the number of people who will buy a brand in the future based on their past experience, (2) the price premium that a brand can generate and justify relative to competitors, and (3) the value of potential brand extensions in the future. Success for building BVA is in the concurrent management of all three components.

Brand value, customer loyalty, and customer repurchase rate can be used as top-tier market metrics in a Six Sigma measurement system. (For more information on Six Sigma business-measurement systems, see Question 44.) Each of these metrics can be linked to the critical-to-quality (CTQ) measures using a mutually exclusive, completely exhaustive (MECE) decomposition of the measurement system following a y = f (x) analysis (see Question 12).

How does a company define its Six Sigma goals?

Goal setting should begin with an organization's business Y's (e.g., shareholder value-added and customer loyalty) because they define success for key stakeholders. Thus, all employees should work together to achieve these goals. But because business Y's represent complex organizational behaviors, not all levels of an organization can influence them directly. Therefore, these measures must be broken down using "drill-down" logic to uncover the areas for investigation in a Six Sigma project.

This drill-down logic uses a sequence of questions to focus a DMAIC analysis on meaningful business issues. This logic describes the $y = f(x)$ analysis of business performance from business Y's to process X's and applies two logical rules to separate the performance factors in the tree diagram below to create an MECE analysis pathway.

A $y = f(x)$ MECE Analysis

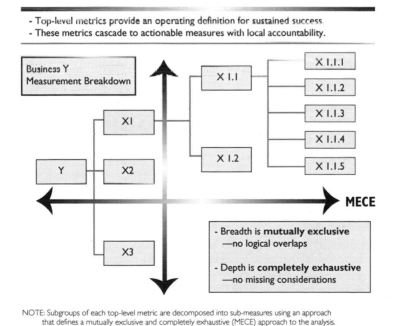

- Top-level metrics provide an operating definition for sustained success.
- These metrics cascade to actionable measures with local accountability.

Business Y Measurement Breakdown

X I.I.I
X I.I
X I.I.2
XI
X I.I.3
X I.I.4
X 1.2
Y
X2
X I.I.5

MECE

- Breadth is **mutually exclusive**
  —no logical overlaps

X3

- Depth is **completely exhaustive**
  —no missing considerations

NOTE: Subgroups of each top-level metric are decomposed into sub-measures using an approach that defines a mutually exclusive and completely exhaustive (MECE) approach to the analysis.

What is MECE?

Mutually exclusive (ME): Logically distinct alternatives that have no overlap in the way they are defined. They have no interactions or confounding with other factors.

Completely exhaustive (CE): A comprehensive description to the lowest level of detail. No significant measurement element is eliminated, and all measures are directly related to the work that people perform.

▶ TIP

The sequence of questions addressed using drill-down logic goes as follows:

- What elements in your business are the ones most critical to quality, as defined by your customers, and not meeting desired performance levels?
- How do you measure performance in this area today?
- What indications do you have that this area needs improvement?
- How do you operationally define a defect in this area?
- Once you discover a defect, where is it observed and when does it occur?
- What factors can be adjusted to improve current performance?
- How much opportunity for improvement exists?
- How can you adjust these factors to improve performance and achieve the best results?

How is an MECE diagram developed?

The creation of an MECE diagram must follow the organizational architecture of the business-measurement system. Typically three levels of organizational performance define a measurement system. These levels are as follows:

❑ **Enterprise-wide.** Metrics used for evaluating the performance of an organization as a whole must reflect the balanced interests of its stakeholders. At this level, capital funds are allocated to grow and strengthen a business, the grand strategy for long-term performance is created, and the Six Sigma Recognize step is implemented. At this level, the key tool to use in creating a measurement system is the balanced scorecard. Both financial and customer elements of the balanced scorecard are cascaded to the business-area level of an organization.

❑ **Business-area level.** This level of organizational performance directly serves customers and markets and is responsible for delivering financial performance and enduring customer value. At this level, a Six Sigma customer dashboard (see definition later in this chapter) is used to focus an organization on areas that can impact customer satisfaction. These areas can be connected to the goals at the enterprise-wide level using an MECE logic tree. In addition, because all these areas are actionable, they can be used to define Six Sigma projects.

At this level, when the Six Sigma Define step is implemented, performance measurements tend to relate directly to the core business processes and indicate defects in the process, cost of the process, and productivity of the process (i.e., cycle time). Master Black Belts and Black Belts create a customer dashboard by using y = f (x) MECE analysis to break down top-tier metrics into actionable measures.

❑ **Work-process level.** This level of organizational performance encompasses the daily work that produces goods and delivers services to customers. At this level, work can be definitively measured in terms of cost, time to perform, and defects relative to standard work requirements. Business must be managed at this level to produce a predictable outcome. All data collected at this level consists of attributes or measured data that can be analyzed with basic statistics.

Balancing the Performance Indicators

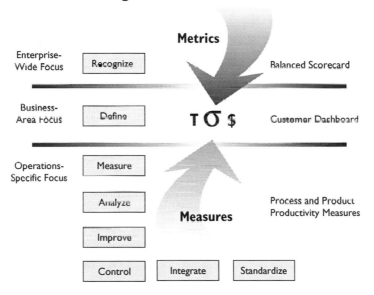

A measurement diagram is built like a tree diagram. It has distinct subordinate branches representing mutually exclusive mathematical relationships. These relationships are broken down into actionable measures that directly relate to the process work that people perform. This type of tree diagram is also called an MECE analysis because there are no logical overlaps among the branches and no missing details. Such a diagram depicts a system of individual measures drilled down from layer to layer by building a logical description of the interrelationships among the measures using a y = f (x) analysis.

Such a drill-down can be described mathematically as a *Markov chain*, a sequence of event measurements that can be represented binomially as success or failure and formed into a probability sequence that logically defines the expected value of success. In Six Sigma this measurement of defect-free outcomes is called the *rolled throughput yield (RTY)*, the probability that a process will produce the desired quality outcome on the first attempt without any rework. This is calculated as the yield of all subprocesses multiplied in a sequence.

NOTE

RTY calculates process performance when the internal defects are known and the defect opportunities can be identified. When an external view of the product is the only possible perspective (e.g., only the customer observes the number of defects in the units delivered), then process sigma can be made using e^{-dpu} as an estimator.

Linking the Measurement System

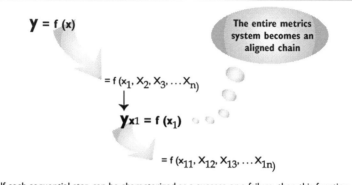

$y = f(x)$

The entire metrics system becomes an aligned chain

$= f(x_1, x_2, x_3, \ldots x_n)$

$y_{x1} = f(x_1)$

$= f(x_{11}, x_{12}, x_{13}, \ldots x_{1n})$

If each sequential step can be characterized as a success or a failure, then this function becomes a Markov process whose probability of successful transition can be calculated using a chain of binomial events to calculate the overall outcome of all "success states."

The tree diagram on the next page illustrates the breakdown of the financial measure known as return on assets. This metric is divided into two mutually exclusive and completely exhaustive logical categories—one dealing with revenue (return) and one dealing with the value of assets. These two factors can then be broken down into mutually exclusive and completely exhaustive categories. Return is broken down into five sources of revenue: sales, service, supplies, support, and passive returns. These can be analyzed by time period, location, and category sub-type to isolate possible problems. The same type of decomposition can be made for the asset categories.

Return-on-Assets Metric Decomposition

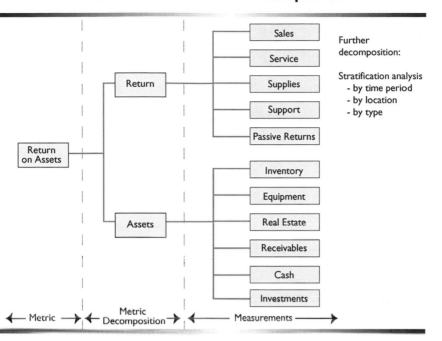

At the point where stratification makes sense, data analysis can be done to determine the location and extent of a problem. In addition, the activities that lead to this performance can be evaluated to find the root cause of observed performance variances.

What is a customer dashboard?

Just as a pilot has many gauges and indicators that describe the performance of an airplane, business leaders have many indicators that define business excellence. The most critical, actionable indicators are placed in front of the pilot's face in a heads-up display to ensure that they catch his/her attention. A similar logic follows when creating a customer dashboard. The set of business Y's are the actionable measures that always must be in the face of management when thinking about delivering top-quality service to customers. The dashboard should have between seven and twelve such metrics. These must be broken down to the action to be taken by the management team at some level using y = f (x) MECE analysis to take corrective action. (See Question 44 for more detail on building such a system.)

How does this help to create goals?

The goals of the organization must be linked from the enterprise-wide level to the work-process level. The linking mechanism is the statistical function described by the breakdown of the business Y's using the MECE y = f (x) analysis. Goals can be set at every level of the organization based on an indicator that is actionable at each level.

Authority must be delegated to regulate this measure at the organizational level so managers can be held accountable. (See Question 5 for an explanation of the three conditions needed to hold people accountable.)

▶ TIP

An organization is ready to build its Six Sigma measurement system once it develops its first Master Black Belts. Typically one or more Master Black Belts are involved in the development and management of the measurement-system design until the system can be translated into an automated information system supported by computer technology.

When the breakdown of the business system occurs, three important analysis pathways are used in the measurement system to set goals for business success. The basic goals of any business are to do the following:

- Increase throughput (i.e., productivity of salable products or services).

- Decrease operating expenses.

- Increase return on assets by reducing inventory and unnecessary assets.

- Provide quality to ensure customer satisfaction.

These goals can be measured using quality, cost, and cycle time, where each has been further broken down to identify its source and magnitude.

The following cost-time profile for a process illustrates where time and cost are consumed in the flow of a work process. Each process step is illustrated as a histogram in two dimensions: cycle time and absolute cost of the process step. A cumulative curve shows the total cost as a percentage of total process costs. (In many cases this might not add up to 100% because some costs are for the process as a whole rather than for the set of steps that define the process.)

Process Cost-Time Profile

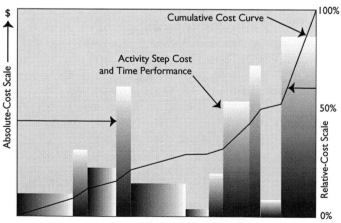

How do I do it?

The business system created around the Six Sigma customer dashboard has many elements that combine to create the goal-setting process. This process also creates management-directed projects that drive the strategic change initiatives of the organization. The following points define the goal-setting process and highlight its linkage to project selection:

❑ **Enterprise model.** This comprehensive model describes how a business operates. It is useful for demonstrating redundancies, needless feedback loops, and exceptionally long processes that might need streamlining to eliminate non-value-added steps.

❑ **Measurement map of MECE y = f (x).** This presentation of the MECE y = f (x) analysis measurement system provides a visual indication of areas where an organization is not meeting its targeted performance.

❑ **Capability analysis.** This describes the current performance of a process by comparing the customer requirement and current variation against the designed process performance (Cpk) calculated as the ratio of the customer requirement for the potential capability (Cp) if the process is centered. When the process is operating under statistical control, Cp and Cpk are used for capability analysis. When it is not operating under statistical control, then the process potential is assessed using capability ratios for Pp and Ppk.

❑ **Baseline analysis.** This is the initial performance profile of a process before any changes are implemented. Performance improvement is typically evaluated against this starting point.

❑ **Benchmarking.** This compares a company's process performance to the best known external performance for the same process. The reasons for the superior external performance must be evaluated.

❑ **Entitlement determination.** The gap between Cp and Cpk is called an entitlement because management has paid to design the process to operate at the Cp level. But variation has degraded the process performance to the Cpk level. Management is entitled to close this performance gap.

❑ **Gap analysis.** This is the analysis of the magnitude of performance between two sets of data (e.g., internal performance versus benchmark, or planned versus actual) with an accompanying analysis of the root cause for the observed gap.

❑ **Goal setting.** In many organizations, goals are set to achieve an improvement of 5% or 10% over prior performance. The goal of a Six Sigma project should be to eliminate as much variation as possible, perhaps as much as two-thirds, to effect a one-sigma or more shift in reduction of defects and to save as much as $250,000 annually. Six Sigma improvement projects should take these numbers and multiply them by the number of projects to be completed to set a proposed quality improvement (sigma level) and cost savings.

❑ **Target deployment.** Specific targets can be designed within an organization to be control points for the deployment of Six Sigma projects. The local process owner is held accountable for delivering the savings and quality improvement after a project is initiated.

Engineering a Business as a System

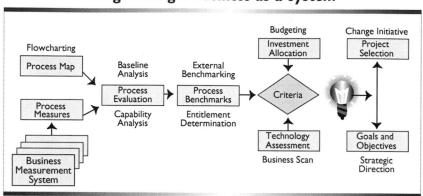

QUESTION

What does a deployment champion do?

A deployment champion serves as the overall implementation coordinator for an organization's Six Sigma initiative. Typically this person reports implementation progress to the Six Sigma steering committee. This person is responsible for scheduling training, ensuring management selects appropriate project champions and Black Belt candidates and trains them properly, tracking progress of improvement projects, and communicating about the Six Sigma initiative and its results to the entire organization. Deployment champions also follow up on Six Sigma project-control plans with the process owner and institutionalize project results by leveraging improvements to all similar business processes. Often a deployment champion also serves as the contract administrator for consulting services related to Six Sigma.

A deployment champion must be a respected representative of the senior management team who is able to influence senior leaders as well as peers. This person must also actively pursue opportunities for continuous improvement and persist in achieving successful conclusions. In large organizations, the job of deployment champion is typically a full-time assignment.

▶ TIP

A Six Sigma deployment champion should exhibit the following characteristics.

- Reliability. Deployment champions must be able to speak frankly to the organization about performance and the need for change without concern for personal or political ramifications. Management can rely on them to reflect their authentic views and communicate their message, despite any difficulty they might encounter. Deployment champions must also be able to address problems that the organization has been unable to resolve in the past and has thus found it convenient to ignore rather than eliminate them.

- Empathy. Deployment champions must have a personal concern for the success of the entire organization, not a narrow functional perspective or global bias. They should determine the value of their contributions to the organization's success by looking at those contributions' long-term impact on the organization's culture and the sustainability of their results when the organization faces challenges from external competition.

- Modesty. Deployment champions focus on the success of their cause or initiative, not on their personal advantage. While they have confidence that they can make a change initiative successful, their ego never gets in the way of achieving the objective. They actively share the glory that comes with successful change. They are personally humble and value all contributors to the change.

- Practicality. Deployment champions judge success by implementation results. They value results rather than change models and implementation plans. They prefer implementation of an 80% solution over waiting for the discovery of a 100% solution. Substantial progress of the organization is more important to them than speaking charismatic words that excite action for only a short duration. Ideally, the deployment champion judges results on a five-year horizon. These are sustainable results that are directly attributable to their contribution to the change initiative.

- Courage. Deployment champions should have a passion for their work that overrides their personal self-protection mechanisms for managing risk. While they are not averse to risk, they don't take senseless risks. They are eager to challenge the appropriateness of the organization's status quo in light of the change initiative.

What do business leaders do?

Business leaders serve as process owners and project champions (see definition below) by setting an organization's strategic direction and overseeing its implementation. Business leaders implement Six Sigma as they manage the changes they plan for the organization. This is not an additional duty or a part-time position. Six Sigma is the methodology by which business leaders deliver their improvement strategy.

Business leaders establish a strategic direction for the company and then execute a sequence of process-improvement projects to achieve that direction. All business-process improvement occurs one project at a time. By managing project definition and coordinating activities across projects, business leaders can focus their organization's resources to accomplish complex objectives. They maintain a strategic focus on what must get done and maintain long-term clarity about their direction to achieve constancy of purpose. Their persistence makes their strategy become a reality.

Business leaders work with Master Black Belts during the Six Sigma Recognize step (see Question 8). Through the formal issuance of a project charter, business leaders hand off authority for a project to the Black Belt during the Six Sigma Define step. As the Black Belt follows the DMAIC process, business leaders monitor the progress and ensure that their business objectives are being followed. Regular progress reviews ensure that business lessons are learned, in addition to process-level lessons that the Black Belt uncovers during the DMAIC process.

Business leaders focus on ensuring that a project delivers business results by serving as project champions or process owners. These roles are defined below.

Project champion. Perhaps the most under-discussed yet most significant role in Six Sigma implementation is that of the project champion, a process owner who provides a business focus for Six Sigma projects. Project champions have the primary responsibility for identifying, selecting, and defining projects on which Black Belts should work in their specific business area. In cooperation with Master Black Belts, project champions perform the Define step in both the DMAIC (see Question 24) and DMADV (see Question 35) processes. Project champions also conduct regular progress reviews at each milestone to ensure that a project meets its intended business objectives. When the process owner also serves as the project champion, that person implements the recommendations resulting from the Six Sigma project.

Project champions are responsible for keeping the Six Sigma program focused within their business area. They select Black Belts, set improvement targets, approve projects, and provide the resources needed to conduct projects. Champions also review projects on a regular basis and are responsible for deployment of Six Sigma and for reinforcing the principles of Six Sigma within their business area. They work with local managers to ensure the financial benefits of Six Sigma projects and serve as mentors to Black Belts.

While Black Belts serve as the analytical engine for Six Sigma projects, a project champion serves as the business catalyst who ensures that projects stay on target and produce results. Perhaps the biggest failure in Six Sigma implementations is the ineffective engagement of the middle managers in meaningful tasks that contribute to the long-term business success of Six Sigma. When this happens, they find it difficult to understand how Six Sigma is a real management initiative. Most companies implementing Six Sigma train all their middle managers to be project champions.

Process owner. A process owner is a line manager responsible for the performance of a specific work process. Process owners maintain the business controls that ensure the consistent performance of their work process according to its targeted deliverable requirements and the associated profit or loss. Because process owners are charged with this responsibility, they have a vested interest in all Six Sigma improvement projects. Process owners must ensure that the resources assigned to a project are effectively applied to improvement areas that matter the most to the organization. Six Sigma projects must satisfy the process owner's priority strategic objectives. Because the implementation of a project should result in improved performance that contributes to bottom-line improvement, the process owner, not the Black Belt, is responsible for the implementation of Six Sigma projects.

A process owner's specific responsibilities often include the following:

- Measure, monitor, and manage process performance.
- Maximize process performance as it contributes to total system performance.
- Maintain process documentation so it accurately reflects the current "as is" process.
- Know what world-class performance is for his/her process.
- Identify process problems and opportunities for improvement.
- Recommend and sponsor Black Belt and Green Belt improvement projects.
- Coordinate his/her process-improvement activities with the activities and preferences of customers, suppliers, and other process owners.

Six Sigma leadership council

Business leaders provide executive oversight for an organization's Six Sigma initiative through a cross-organizational leadership council. Typically an executive sponsor heads this team, and the deployment champion serves as its recording secretary. General activities of a leadership council include the following:

- Setting expectations for Six Sigma deployment.
- Ensuring organizational resources are allocated as required for Six Sigma projects.

- Conducting performance reviews of full-time Six Sigma participants to ensure they are adequately managed.
- Communicating results of the Six Sigma initiative to peers.
- Establishing long-term strategies for integrating Six Sigma with mainstream business activities, particularly the strategic-planning process.
- Ensuring that project results and lessons learned are shared with the entire organization.

How do I do it?

Some of the above general ideas can be applied to the specific activities of business leaders in the following ways:

1. Clarify and communicate how Six Sigma drives attainment of strategic business goals.

2. Include discussion about Six Sigma in every business meeting, focusing on how Six Sigma drives business results and the benefits seen to date.

3. During meetings with individual direct reports, discuss your support for the initiative and inquire how they will manage to implement it in their area of responsibility.

4. Make resource decisions to free up your best people to serve as Black Belts.

5. Meet monthly with project champions to discuss what is being learned and any barriers to implementation and to encourage acceleration of their efforts.

6. Ensure that appropriate goals for Six Sigma are included in all performance reviews at all levels of the organization.

7. Incorporate the Six Sigma measurement system and customer dashboard into the organization's operational reporting systems.

8. Recognize people with Six Sigma competencies through career counseling and promotion.

What do Black Belts do?

A Black Belt fulfills the analysis role in Six Sigma improvement and innovation projects. He/she leads improvement-project teams and conducts the detailed analysis required for the DMAIC and DMADV methodologies. This person must be able to pursue a problem to find its root cause despite any political pressures or absence of data, and he/she must be able to convince others that his/her data analyses are correct. The role of the Black Belt, the most visible role in a Six Sigma initiative, is critical in Six Sigma implementations.

Black Belt candidates go through an intensive four-week training program in statistical problem solving in the context of the DMAIC approach to problem resolution. They develop technical and managerial skills through this training and from on-the-job personal development. Black Belts must be able to work with front-line employees to discover answers to issues that plague process performance and result in inefficiency. They also help the management team identify an approach that will resolve the problems presented to them. In addition, Black Belts can serve as instructors for their project-team members and educate Green Belts about the tools and methods of Six Sigma.

Black Belts are not responsible for the implementation of a solution. This role is better left for a line manager or process owner.

Expectations for Black Belts

Black Belts should serve a two-year tenure and complete eight to ten projects during this time. If their projects are carefully selected, they experience the breadth and depth of the problems their organization confronts and learn the critical-thinking skills necessary to become a general manager.

Typically, Black Belt candidates are college graduates who have at least three years' experience at their company, which ensures their ability to work with a wide variety of managers. Other characteristics that successful Black Belt candidates possess are listed below.

❑ **Will to win.** Candidates have a high level of enthusiasm for improved company performance, are proactive, can operate without continual supervision, and demonstrate tenacity in overcoming resistance to new ideas.

❑ **Mathematical acumen.** Candidates are confident working with basic mathematics, graphical analysis methods, and business models. They are not fearful of statistics.

- ❑ **Stress management.** Candidates cope well in stressful situations and under intense time pressure, bring clarity to ambiguous problems, and know how to set goals, establish priorities, and focus their activities to achieve them.

- ❑ **Interpersonal savvy.** Candidates are able to work with diverse groups of people. They develop constructive relationships at all levels of the organization, use tact appropriately, and can diffuse high-tension situations comfortably.

- ❑ **Problem-solving skills/analytical thinking.** Candidates use rigorous logic and methods to solve difficult problems, probe all fruitful sources for solutions, and look beyond the obvious for constructive solutions.

- ❑ **Quick to learn.** Candidates are open to changes in work methods, analyze successes and failures for improvement ideas, and enjoy the challenge of unfamiliar tasks.

In addition, personal development in the following areas can enhance candidate effectiveness.

- ❑ **Innovation management.** Candidates are good at encouraging others to come up with creative ideas, and they make good judgments about which ideas are worth pursuing. They can assess how creative ideas will operate when implemented.

- ❑ **Customer focus.** Candidates are dedicated to finding out what customers want. They know how to gain the cooperation, respect, and trust of customers.

- ❑ **Presentation skills.** Candidates present information concisely in a way that provides people with the information they need to facilitate appropriate decisions.

- ❑ **Communication skills.** Candidates possess good verbal and written communication skills.

- ❑ **Leadership skills.** Candidates can establish what needs to be done and then build a collaborative work environment within the team to ensure it will operate together well and achieve its objective. They hold people accountable for the quality of their work.

- ❑ **Planning skills.** Candidates manage projects well. They estimate with accuracy the length and difficulty of activities, break down work into process steps, set goals, develop schedules, assign tasks, anticipate problems and roadblocks, measure performance against goals, and evaluate performance.

- ❑ **Personal computer skills.** Candidates possess basic computer skills and have experience with core software, including a graphical drawing program.

Black Belt training

The Black Belt training program combines the classroom and the workplace. A practical project demonstrates how analytical methods apply to a real-world environment. This training period is orchestrated into five steps that follow the DMAIC steps of the analysis process. Each step begins with a management review of project performance and includes classroom training, project activity to demonstrate tool use, and a technical review to ensure learning has been transferred from the classroom to the project appropriately. Black Belts are coached to use computer aids for process mapping, statistical analysis, simulation analysis, project management, and reporting.

When the project is completed, the organization's finance group should conduct an independent project review that ensures the claims for financial gains are warranted and follow the company's accepted set of accounting practices.

How do I do it?

The Black Belt nomination process should be a positive recognition experience for each nominated employee. The following process is used at one major corporation:

1. Screen the list of high-potential employees and group them into categories according to their background: engineering, science, and mathematics in one category; business, marketing, and commerce in a second category; and all others in a third category.

2. Rank the employees in each category according to performance by quartile to indicate their performance relative to their peers.

3. Determine the number of Black Belts to be trained, distribution of Black Belts by business process and functional area, and requirements for Black Belts developed by the business leaders in your organization who support the Six Sigma initiative.

4. Identify enough Black Belt candidates from the top two quartiles to fill the training requirements and match Black Belts to business leaders who will serve as their mentors and project champions. Business leaders should notify each candidate's immediate manager of the nomination and the priority that this position has over all other work of the organization.

5. Develop a communication package so that communications to potential Black Belts are standardized. All receive the same message about the importance of the Black Belt position, duration of the assignment, benefits to their career, requirements for certification, and performance expectations.

6. Develop a nomination letter, preferably signed by the organization's CEO, to send to Black Belt candidates to ask them to consider taking on this position.

7. Identify a point of contact where candidates can call to discuss Six Sigma and the Black Belt position and find more information.

8. Prepare an assessment of mathematical confidence to overcome the anxiety that many candidates might feel about intensive statistical training. A good resource to use is the book *Using Business Statistics: A Guide for Beginners* by Terry Dickey (Crisp Publications, 1995).

9. Send nomination letters. The business leader and the deployment champion make follow-up phone calls to answer questions and remove any roadblocks from each candidate's path toward development as a Black Belt.

▶ TIP

Managers might object to the solicitation of their best employees to become Black Belts. When this happens, senior business leaders or executive sponsors should discuss the precedence of the Six Sigma program over all other work that the organization is doing and communicate its long-term strategic value. Although a no net-additional-headcount (no-net-add) policy goes hand-in-hand with a Six Sigma implementation, this does not mean that Black Belt candidates' regular positions should go unfilled. Rather, this is an opportunity for local managers to develop other high-potential employees by assigning them the candidates' usual challenging work. This way, even more employees receive career-enhancing opportunities.

QUESTION  **16**

Why is a formal
project charter important?

One readiness factor for Six Sigma is an organization's ability to properly define project scope. Three criteria define the probability for a Six Sigma project's success: availability of data, frequency of process cycles, and number of organizations involved in a decision-making capacity. After a business problem is assessed for these factors, a project charter must be prepared by the project champion, Master Black Belt, Black Belt, and the process owners affected by the project. Management then approves the charter.

A management-approved project charter enables the Black Belt to more rapidly convince the organization of the legitimacy of the work without going through a full rationalization of the problem each time a new area or person becomes involved. It also allows the Black Belt to search for sources of process variation. A charter is used at regular project reviews to update resource requirements (such as measurement systems or test time on production operations) and to identify project participants, their roles, and their expected level of involvement. Project charters are also used to identify project-management measures, such as completion statistics and results achieved.

How do I do it?

The first step in developing a charter is to define the business reason for a project and its potential improvement opportunity. Business leaders must select and define Black Belt projects that have a strategic priority for the organization. Step two is to determine the current state performance and best short-term performance of the process in question and to obtain an external benchmark to determine how good its performance could be. Step three is to estimate the potential benefit from closing the gap between current and ideal performance and to identify how closing this gap will contribute to achievement of the organization's business strategy. Business leaders then assign individuals to serve as project champion and Black Belt, and they identify team members. The fourth step is to fill in the charter form and discuss it with the Black Belt prior to formal approval.

A charter might change several times as a project develops and new information is obtained. A project charter must be finalized by the end of the Analyze step of the DMAIC process. (See Question 26 for more information.)

What is included in a project charter? The following sample provides a guide:

Project Charter Format

Page 1

SIX SIGMA PROJECT—TEAM CHARTER

Project Name:
Project Number:

Project Name, Date:
Department/Business Unit:
Date Project Initiated:
Date Charter Last Revised:
Team Mission:

Improvement Opportunity:

Initial Potential Benefit Estimate:

Business Reason for Interest:

Project Scope:

Strategic Alignment:

Key Customers:

Page 2

Team Structure:
Executive Sponsor:
Process Owner/Project Champion:
Team Leader:
Black Belt:
Team Members:

Process Flow, Key Metrics, Defect Definition:

Process Optimization/Input Targets:

Performance Objectives/Output Targets:

Key Challenges:

Key Milestones:
Complete M:
Complete A:
Complete I:
Complete C:
Realization Review:
Project Sign-Off:

QUESTION

How does a company choose a successful training project?

A natural tension exists between the desires of business leaders and those of Black Belts regarding an initial Six Sigma project assignment. Business leaders want to demonstrate that Six Sigma works in their business environment and accelerate its acceptance. They want a project that offers a significant potential benefit and that results in recommendations that are easily implemented. Business leaders also want to resolve chronic problems. The natural tendency of management, therefore, is to initially define project scope broadly.

Black Belts, on the other hand, want a project with low complexity, lots of available data, susceptibility to the demonstration of statistical tools, and the ability to be completed during the four-month training period. The natural tendency of Black Belts, then, is to initially define project scope narrowly.

▶ TIP

Business leaders can use the following simplified process for initial project selection. First, they decide what criteria to use for evaluating projects. Next, they brainstorm a list of chronic problems and process areas needing improvement. This list can also include areas identified as opportunities for improvement in ISO 9000 audits or Baldrige-based self-assessments. They then create a Microsoft Excel matrix (with criteria on one axis and projects on the other) and use multivoting to determine the priority of the projects. (See *The Memory Jogger II*™ for more information about multivoting.)

How does an organization objectively select a Black Belt training project that satisfies these two divergent desires simultaneously?

Training projects should be defined within the scope of a strategically important concern for the business. Business leaders should look at core business processes with poor quality (i.e., low sigma levels) and large operating costs to find problem areas. They also must consider the ability to replicate business-improvement opportunities across multiple business units (e.g., retail units, production lines, or workers with the same job description). Business leaders must keep in mind that solutions requiring changes to human behavior are more difficult to implement than those requiring changes to documentation, forms, or computer software.

Good Six Sigma training projects for new Black Belts have three characteristics:

1. They are limited either in scope or in the number of processes directly affected by the project.

2. There is frequent process repetition, so change can be observed and data collection can be done efficiently.

3. Enough data is available for analysis.

Prospective Black Belt training projects can be tested for these three dimensions using a multi-criteria decision-support tool called the Analytic Hierarchy Process (AHP), developed by Thomas L. Saaty.

How do I do it?

AHP provides a logical approach for making a complex decision by presenting a problem in a hierarchical structure and using pairwise comparisons of management's decision criteria to determine trade-offs among the objectives and find the most appropriate choice. AHP evaluates options according to the same criteria, which are weighted for importance to the decision maker. This approach follows a three-step process, which is explained below.

1. Structure the decision problem in a hierarchy.

Analytic Hierarchy Process (AHP)

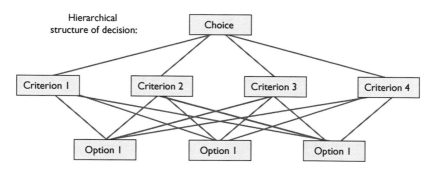

2. Compare the alternatives and the criteria. These comparisons are made in pairs with respect to each element of the next-highest level. To establish relative comparisons, the following scale can be used to translate verbal descriptors into numerical values.

Establishing Relative Comparisons

Assignment of scores for verbal descriptions of strength in the pairwise comparisons:

Verbal Scale	Numerical Value
Equally important, likely or preferred	1
Moderately more important, likely or preferred	3
Strongly more important, likely or preferred	5
Very strongly more important, likely or preferred	7
Extremely more important, likely or preferred	9
NOTE: Intermediate values are used to reflect compromises by the decision maker.	2, 4, 6, 8

3. Synthesize the comparisons to derive the priorities for all the alternatives with respect to each decision criterion and the relative weighting of each criterion with respect to the desired choice. The local priorities are then multiplied by the weights of the respective criteria. The results are summed to get the overall priority of each alternative and determine the final rank order of all decision options.

Pairwise Comparison of Options

	Option 1	Option 2	Option 3	Local Priority
Option 1				
Option 2				
Option 3				

Compare each criterion pairwise with respect to the choice:

Pairwise Comparison of Decision Criteria

	Criterion 1	Criterion 2	Criterion 3	Criterion 4	Weights
Criterion 1					
Criterion 2					
Criterion 3					
Criterion 4					

List the priorities, weights, and final ranking of the options:

Criteria Weighting

	Criterion 1 (Weight)	Criterion 2 (Weight)	Criterion 3 (Weight)	Criterion 4 (Weight)	Global Priority	Rank Order
Option 1						
Option 2						
Option 3						

Finally, conduct a sensitivity study of the final ranking to evaluate the impact of a single criterion on the final choice.

EXAMPLE

There are three criteria for deciding which project to select. Each has three performance levels.

1. Transaction-process frequency. High = hourly, medium = monthly, low = annually.

2. Process scope. Broad = entire organization, medium = three different groups, narrow = single group.

3. Data availability. High = recorded frequently for a long duration, medium = recorded monthly for less than three years, low = recorded annually for less than three years.

When there are three projects, each should be ranked using the criteria to evaluate its acceptability for a Black Belt training project. This will result in the following data matrix of projects versus criteria:

Process Data

	Transaction Frequency	Process Scope	Data Availability
Project A	Annual	Enterprise	Low
Project B	Monthly	Finance	Medium
Project C	Daily	Service	High

The following improvement projects are considered:

- Project A = Strategic-planning process
- Project B = Cash-management process
- Project C = Product-service process

The following pairwise comparisons among these three factors are considered for the three projects:

Pairwise Comparisons of Decision Criteria

Process Scope	A	B	C
Project A	I	.5	.25
Project B	.25	I	7
Project C	9	5	I

Transaction Frequency	A	B	C
Project A	I	.5	.25
Project B	.5	I	9
Project C	9	.5	I

Data Availability	A	B	C
Project A	I	.5	.25
Project B	.5	I	2
Project C	4	2	I

The first table implies that each project relative to itself is neutrally weighted. However, if project A is compared to projects B and C, the monthly and daily transaction frequencies are valued more highly. The scale used for the pairwise comparison is based on the scores presented in the figure titled "Establishing Relative Comparisions," extended to a partial-point scale to represent less-than-favorable comparisons. Similar analyses are performed for process scope and data availability.

Evaluate the importance of the three criteria using a similar pairwise comparison to determine factor weights:

Criteria Weighting

	Transaction Frequency	Process Scope	Data Availability	Raw Weight	Relative Weight
Transaction Frequency	I	3	5	8.00/15.99	0.50
Process Scope	.33	I	5	6.33/15.99	0.396
Data Availability	.16	.5	I	1.66/15.99	0.104

Determine the raw scores of the project options by adding the scores from each criterion for the project comparisons and divide by the sum for the entire comparison:

Comparative Assessment

Raw Priority	Transaction Frequency	Process Scope	Data Availability
Project A	.064	.067	.143
Project B	.385	.333	.286
Project C	.550	.600	.571

The final analysis combines these weighted scores to determine the overall ranking using the following process:

Determine the weighted score of the project options by multiplying the raw priority by the factor weights and then ranking the projects.

Factor	Transaction Frequency	Process Scope	Data Availability	Score	Rank
Project A	.50 × .064 = .032	.396 × 0.67 = .265	.104 × .143 = .015	.312	3
Project B	.50 × .385 = .193	.396 × .333 = .132	.104 × .286 = .030	.355	2
Project C	.50 × .550 = .275	.396 × .600 = .238	.104 × .571 = .059	.572	1

Based on this analysis, the best project to select would be C, improving the product-service process.

▶ **TIP**

One way to simplify this problem is to concentrate on or ignore one of the variables. Perhaps the best variable on which to concentrate is transaction frequency. This is done by selecting only those processes whose transaction frequency is one month or less.

▶ **TIP**

Another simplification technique is to disallow any projects that require capital investment. These tend to be DMADV projects and do not have the same ability to showcase the use of the DMAIC toolkit. Also, the objective of a capital project is to seek a higher level of design-process capability (Cpk), while the purpose of a training project should be to move the observed process capability (Cp) to the design level (Cpk).

▶ **TIP**

Another potential application of the AHP method is in the selection of Black Belts and Master Black Belts.

How should Black Belts account for savings?

Project return is not always evident to the inexperienced Black Belt. To help Black Belts understand the potential benefits of a project, business leaders can use a set of financial rules to improve the bottom-line focus. Some basic rules common to Six Sigma deployments include the following:

❏ Divide the benefits from the project into recurring benefits (ones that are permanently taken out of the operating budget) and non-recurring benefits (ones that are one-time savings). The organization's finance department should provide guidelines for the cost of relevant salaries and benefits. This department should be actively involved in Six Sigma projects throughout the deployment period (see Question 32)

❏ Discriminate between hard (auditable) and soft (subjective) benefits from the project.

❏ Count only a full year's recurring hard benefit as the project's basic return. Add the cost of capital effect for any one-time savings (typically 10% of the one-time savings) and subtract the cost of analysis (i.e., salaries and benefits of the Black Belt and Master Black Belt who dedicate time to the project) and implementation expenses.

❏ All project savings must be validated by the finance department.

What is the fundamental difference between hard and soft benefits? Soft benefits include improvement that reduces the "irritant factor" for employees doing the work, improves customer satisfaction, avoids unbudgeted costs, and/or reduces the workload of individuals without reducing staffing requirements or the demand for temporary workers. Hard benefits include reduction in cash payments to external parties, lower costs for non-value-added work, improved productivity that is salable to the market, and other forms of measurable revenue growth. In addition, any benefit that reduces the need for assets, eliminates the need for organizational infrastructure, or reduces working capital can also be considered a hard benefit.

Calculate the benefit of a Six Sigma project that reduces a process's asset requirement by $1 million, eliminates three positions (where salary and benefits are valued at $100,000 per person) and improves productivity by 500 units per month for a product with insufficient market supply (revenue per unit is $10).

First, the allowed asset benefit would be the cost of capital multiplied by the asset reduction (10% of $1 million, or $100,000). The benefit from head-count reduction would be $300,000, and the benefit from the improved productivity would be $5,000 per month for twelve months ($60,000). Thus, the benefit estimate for this project is $460,000.

All these benefits are hard benefits, with two caveats. The first is that if the head count is not reduced, it becomes a hard benefit that was not captured (i.e., a soft benefit). Business leaders must then find out why there was no reduction in head count to go along with the reduction in work. The second caveat is that all products must be salable to count as a hard benefit.

▶ TIP

There must be only one scorekeeper for financial results. It is appropriate for this person to be appointed by the organization's chief financial officer. Typically this role goes to an individual who is trained as a champion or Black Belt.

▶ TIP

To maximize the benefits from Six Sigma projects, Black Belts need to work with their Master Black Belts and business leaders to find opportunities to apply their project findings to other parts of the organization. All resulting benefits can be accrued to the original Black Belt project, since it was the original source of the potential benefit to the organization.

What goes into a Six Sigma deployment plan?

A good deployment plan includes all the details required for a successful Six Sigma implementation. It serves as a historical document to preserve decisions made about the implementation and as a plan for future actions to be taken. Subjects covered in a deployment plan include the following:

❑ **Vision and mission statement.** Records how the Six Sigma initiative relates to the vision and mission of the organization.

❑ **Cultural alignment.** Describes linkages among the organization's cultural values before the Six Sigma initiative and any effects the initiative might have on the culture through either reinforcement or directional changes.

❑ **Critical measures and metrics.** This section of the deployment plan documents the measurement architecture of the organization from the top-tier business Y's to the daily management X's. It is typically not created until the organization has trained and deployed its first Master Black Belts.

❑ **Goals and improvement objectives.** This section describes the goals and objectives of the organization's Six Sigma initiative and how they align with its strategic objectives.

❑ **Roles, responsibilities, and organizational structure.** This section describes the general roles and assignment of responsibilities to the organization's business leaders for the deployment of Six Sigma.

❑ **Business-leader role definition.** Describes what is expected of the project champion and process owner.

❑ **Black Belt selection criteria and job description.** Defines the selection criteria and performance expectations for Black Belts and provides a job description for this full-time position.

❑ **Master Black Belt selection criteria and job description.** Defines the selection criteria and performance expectations for Master Black Belts and provides a job description for this full-time position.

❑ **Green Belt selection criteria and job description.** Defines the selection criteria and performance expectations for Green Belts.

❑ **Rewards, recognition, and achievement program.** Outlines policies and procedures that human resources must implement for recognition and reward to reinforce the Six Sigma initiative.

- **Training resources, materials tailoring, and schedule.** Describes the resources available for training; provides a description of the training programs for business leaders, Black Belts, and Green Belts; and promotes the training schedule for course offerings.

- **Evaluation process.** Describes how Black Belts and Master Black Belts will be evaluated for their performance in these positions and expectations for the completion of projects. Typically, expectations are set for these two full-time Six Sigma positions only.

- **Performance-based certification policy.** Defines the certification program for Black Belt qualification. Typically, this includes satisfactory completion of the four-week training program, a training project, and an independent post-training project. Some organizations also have a qualification examination; others offer additional courses in leadership, presentation skills, and the lean enterprise to enrich the basic program.

- **Benchmarking and process baseline measurement work plan.** Describes the plan for conducting external benchmarking studies and internal baseline measurements to define the performance gaps that Six Sigma projects might be able to close.

- **Quality data system definition.** Describes how the measurement system will be implemented, using information-system technology, to gather, analyze, and report on the organization's business Y metrics. This system must also support the diagnostic analysis of the business Y's to the level of the daily management X's if any unacceptable variation is observed in performance.

- **Communication plan.** Describes the requirements for communication, including messages, type of media to be used, and frequency of communication.

- **Project-review process.** Describes the tollgate reviews made for all Six Sigma projects by local management (at each milestone for DMAIC and DMADV) and by senior management (for the commitment of resources and capture of benefits).

- **Improvement budgeting process.** Describes what the organization will do with the benefits received from Six Sigma. Examples include returning the training and consulting investment to the original budget, paying back the investment in the salaries and benefits of employees involved in Six Sigma projects, setting aside funds for investment in revenue-growth opportunities to fund DMADV projects, and/or reducing prices to customers.

- **Labor-reduction policies and process.** Describes how the organization will deal with employee staffing reductions that might occur as a result of Six Sigma projects. This includes policy considerations such as how to manage unbudgeted severance expenses so that local managers do not have a disincentive for downsizing when the work that is eliminated is non-value-adding.

- **Business-system integration.** Defines the enterprise map for each business area or the plan for its development. Identifies work processes and includes a plan to integrate common business and work processes across the organization.

❑ **Six Sigma leadership council charter.** Documents the work procedures for the senior leadership team charged with providing oversight for the Six Sigma initiative. Includes identification of opportunities for Six Sigma projects, procedures for performance reviews, and integration of business-operation enhancement with the plan for continuous improvement of all major organizational areas. The deployment champion, who is normally the secretary or facilitator of this committee, documents all decisions made during council meetings and distributes them to senior managers company-wide.

▶ **TIP**

Many items in the above list (e.g., job descriptions, labor policies for job reduction, and recognitions/rewards) can be developed during business-leader training sessions as workshops that focus on particular decisions. Other items, such as business-system integration and critical measures and metrics, are appropriate for Black Belt projects. Typically an organization's deployment champion is charged with the development and execution of its Six Sigma deployment plan. Reviews are conducted by the senior management team (leadership council or Six Sigma executive steering committee; see Question 14) to ensure smooth implementation of the plan.

Performance Expectations

An "average" Black Belt should complete three to five projects annually for an expected return of $1 million in savings. Master Black Belts can mentor and coach up to ten Black Belts and complete one to three projects annually. These financial expectations must be scaled in accordance with company size, throughput volume, and currency considerations.

How is a Six Sigma deployment scheduled?

An organization-wide deployment of Six Sigma typically has three phases. During the first phase, the architecture for Six Sigma is established. Executives are trained, objectives are determined, customization of the deployment occurs, an initial workshop is conducted with business leaders to define specific parameters for deployment, and a pilot training program for Black Belts is initiated to build a set of case studies for business-leader training. The second phase of deployment occurs after a management briefing about the intent of the senior team and summaries of the case studies conducted in the pilot training program. This phase consists of "waves" of training for business leaders and Black Belts. The third phase is the renewal phase, during which Black Belts are replaced and return to their normal jobs within the organization.

The speed of a Six Sigma implementation is determined by the number of waves of Black Belts trained and the process used to obtain Black Belt candidates from all areas of the organization. The effectiveness of a Six Sigma program is a function of the number of trained Black Belts working full-time on projects. Only when a project's process-improvement recommendations are implemented can its benefits be captured as bottom-line returns.

▶ **TIP**

Always train business leaders first so they can develop a good project for the initial training. This helps to eliminate problems during the Black Belt candidates' first experience with Six Sigma. It also improves the quality of project reviews and the speed of the implementation of project recommendations.

▶ **TIP**

The general rule of thumb is to have one Black Belt developed for every 100 full-time employees of an organization. However, the replacement rate for Black Belts is not the same as the initial deployment rate. During the first two years of a Six Sigma deployment, most of the Black Belt projects use the DMAIC method to eliminate existing problems, capture lost process capability, and improve the productivity of processes. After this has been accomplished, the emphasis shifts to DMADV projects to extend process capability, grow sales revenue, and work outside the organization with critical members of the supply chain on both the customer and supplier sides.

What does the involvement of Black Belts look like over the long term? Consider the following illustration as typical of a Six Sigma deployment, where the number of Black Belts trained is a function of the organization's total work force:

Black Belt Replacement Strategy

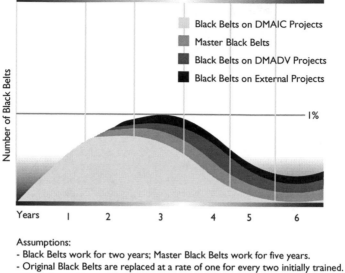

Assumptions:
- Black Belts work for two years; Master Black Belts work for five years.
- Original Black Belts are replaced at a rate of one for every two initially trained.
- There is one Master Black Belt for every ten Black Belts.
- After two years, an organization's Six Sigma focus shifts to DMADV and external projects with customers and suppliers.

How do I do it?

Two factors drive the progress of a Six Sigma deployment: the number of Black Belts trained and the speed at which they are deployed. Once an organization determines these factors, the deployment plan must identify the source of Black Belt candidates for training based on an analysis of the organization and a projection of the need for Black Belts. The maximum number of students for each training wave is twenty-five. The combination of a business-leader seminar (for project champions and process owners) and a Black Belt course represents one wave of training.

The implementation of a Six Sigma initiative typically occurs in two phases. The first focuses on executive orientation, deployment planning, baseline performance measurement of the organization to fix the sigma level of key business processes, pilot training, and customization of the training materials. It culminates with the official launch of the Six Sigma initiative. This phase has four major activities, as described in the following diagram:

Implementation Roll-Out

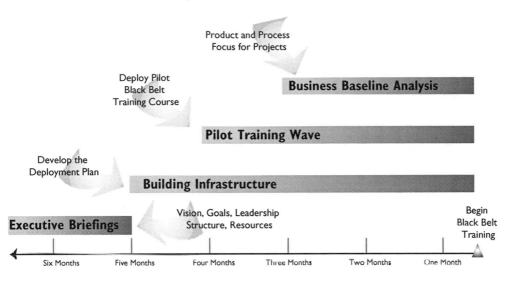

Product and Process
Focus for Projects

Business Baseline Analysis

Deploy Pilot
Black Belt
Training Course

Pilot Training Wave

Develop the
Deployment Plan

Building Infrastructure

Vision, Goals, Leadership
Structure, Resources

Begin
Black Belt
Training

Executive Briefings

| Six Months | Five Months | Four Months | Three Months | Two Months | One Month |

The content of the deployment plan (see Question 19) defines the second phase of a Six Sigma implementation. In this phase, the emphasis shifts from planning to training and project work. Waves of training courses are given to project champions, process owners, and Black Belts.

Black Belts must have access to a Master Black Belt (either internal or external) for support and guidance. Without this support, Black Belts might not achieve their expected project-completion rate of three to five projects per year, and the quality of their projects might suffer from the lack of technical reviews.

Each Black Belt candidate is expected to complete a business-improvement project as an integral part of the four-month training program. Each stage of the training lasts one month and includes a planning period during which the Black Belt meets with the project champion and process owner to conduct a review of the project to keep it on track with its business objectives (see Question 29). It also includes a week of classroom training, during which projects are reviewed with the instructor/Master Black Belt and new methods are presented for the next stage of training. The remainder of each stage is dedicated to on-the-job training by working on an assigned project.

At the completion of Black Belt training, each candidate is expected to demonstrate knowledge and understanding of the use and application of the core Six Sigma toolkit. Black Belts demonstrate their practical ability to use the DMAIC method during the completion of their project. During project work, they work with a team of business leaders and front-line employees to define and resolve a key business issue. Some organizations add further requirements, such as an end-of-course examination that demonstrates the skills attained or a leadership training course that supplements the core curriculum. Black Belt training pursues the schedule shown in the following figure.

Guided Deployment Roll-Out

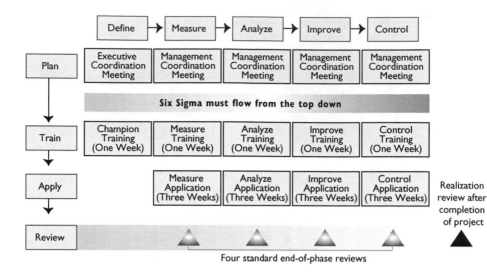

Four standard end-of-phase reviews

How does a company develop a sound communication strategy?

What must management communicate to an organization about Six Sigma, and how should it be done to achieve the best acceptance? One major component of such communication is success sharing. By sharing the success of Six Sigma projects, management reinforces that Six Sigma and its analytical approach is appropriate for the organization, celebrates accomplishments of project teams, reinforces the value of Six Sigma to managers, and promotes communication about Six Sigma within the organization. Success sharing can take many forms, from full reports posted on a company intranet to articles published in a company newsletter.

Another major component of communication about Six Sigma is keeping process owners informed about successful Six Sigma projects in related areas and about their need to apply the results in their areas as well. This enables the organization to achieve savings company-wide.

However, successes are only part of a sound communication strategy. Other messages that must be transmitted to the organization include the following:

▶ Business reasons for implementing Six Sigma.

▶ Alignment of Six Sigma with the organization's culture.

▶ Goals set by management for Six Sigma implementation.

▶ Strategy for roll-out and related roles and responsibilities.

▶ Policy for improvements regarding potential downsizing.

▶ Recognition of good project-team efforts and benefits captured.

A communication strategy should also outline the primary communication channel for each message and secondary channels for reinforcement. Some appropriate communication channels include:

▶ Annual report

▶ Strategic briefings and business reviews

▶ Company-wide meetings

▶ Company newsletters

- Blanket e-mails to employees
- Company web site
- Internal surveys

How do I do it?

A communication strategy can be as simple as a matrix that defines the messages to be transmitted and the communication vehicles to be used. The strategy should also define each message so the intended meaning is clear.

▶ TIP

Disclosing to the public (e.g., at shareholder meetings or professional conferences) that your organization has implemented Six Sigma might negatively impact your stock performance. Many analysts know that a large company usually trains 1% of its work force to be Black Belts and that each Black Belt creates a bottom-line savings of $1 million annually (doing three to five projects for an average savings of $250,000 each). Based on this, analysts might change their expectations of a company's performance when they learn it has implemented Six Sigma.

However, an organization's roll-out plan might not be as aggressive, the number of Black Belts might differ, the organization might achieve a different savings average, or it might have already factored the savings into its financial forecasts. The best communication strategy to the public about Six Sigma is for an organization to let its performance speak for itself. But a CEO can use a potential negative impact on the organization's stock performance to urge Black Belts and business leaders to enable the organization to meet the rising expectations of analysts.

How does quality relate to Six Sigma?

Six Sigma is not just a quality process; it is a business process that can be applied across the entire enterprise using quality methods to achieve business objectives. How is quality addressed in a Six Sigma program?

Quality is defined as the value entitlement of customers, which is formed in two stages. In the first stage, the value entitlement is maximized when the real need of customers is understood and properly translated into a market promise made by the organization (as either a product specification or a service guarantee). In the second stage, the value entitlement is maximized when the product or service consistently achieves its promise as a minimum level of routine performance.

This framework for defining quality presents three potential opportunities for failure to achieve the desired outcome. They represent three different risks in a business model of the organization. They are as follows:

❑ **Producer's risk (type I defect).** A defect that occurs when the producer makes a product in a way that does not meet its market promise.

❑ **Consumer's risk (type II defect).** A defect that occurs when the consumer's real need is not understood and the wrong product is designed for the market.

❑ **Shareholder's risk (type III defect).** A defect that occurs when the wrong product is made for the market, and it is not made according to its market promise.

Managed risk is a situation where management pursues business-development options to minimize risks while at the same time taking advantage of the best opportunities. In this situation, management must decide its tolerance for risk.

Three Types of Risks

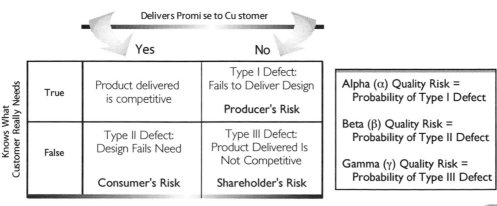

| | | Delivers Promise to Customer | |
		Yes	No
Knows What Customer Really Needs	True	Product delivered is competitive	Type I Defect: Fails to Deliver Design **Producer's Risk**
	False	Type II Defect: Design Fails Need **Consumer's Risk**	Type III Defect: Product Delivered Is Not Competitive **Shareholder's Risk**

Alpha (α) Quality Risk = Probability of Type I Defect

Beta (β) Quality Risk = Probability of Type II Defect

Gamma (γ) Quality Risk = Probability of Type III Defect

This approach to quality follows "value-chain" thinking; that is, value is added from the time a product or service is first conceived through its delivery to customers. In this approach, the factors that are critical to customer satisfaction must be identified and turned into a promise of service delivery or of product performance, called a market offering. This design must be consistently delivered on a routine basis by front-line employees who manage the daily work of the organization. In this approach, quality is a value entitlement of the customer; in other words, customers are entitled to the value that they desire.

Two potential gaps can inhibit the delivery of this value. In the first gap is the Type II defect, and in the second gap is the Type I defect, as illustrated in the figure below.

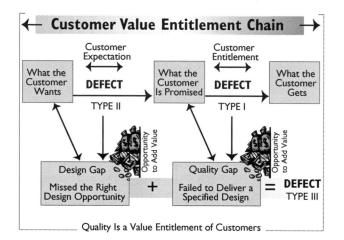

This model for quality is well aligned with Six Sigma. The DMAIC problem-solving method works to close gaps created by a Type I defect (where there is a large gap between Cpk and the design Cp). DMADV is used to drive innovation and ensure that a Type II defect does not occur.

What is the DMAIC problem-solving process?

DMAIC is Six Sigma's rigorous approach for statistical problem solving.

DMAIC: Problem Solving in Six Sigma

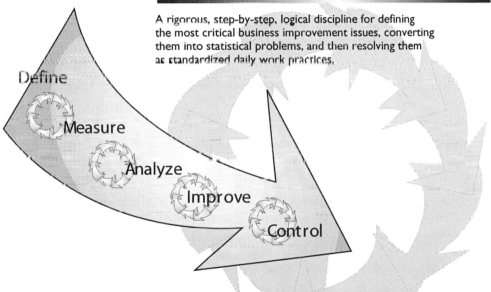

A rigorous, step-by-step, logical discipline for defining the most critical business improvement issues, converting them into statistical problems, and then resolving them as standardized daily work practices.

Define

Measure

Analyze

Improve

Control

The sequential use of probing questions, analytical methods, and specific business knowledge to discover solutions that drive significant performance gains in important operating dimensions.

The term *DMAIC* is an acronym for the process's five sequential steps: Define, Measure, Analyze, Improve, and Control. The DMAIC process involves taking a business problem, translating it into a statistical problem, resolving the statistical problem, and returning a practical solution that is then placed under statistical monitoring and control. The specific activities for these steps are described in detail below.

Define

During this step, the project champion, process owner, and Master Black Belt work with the Black Belt to accomplish the following:

❑ Translate a current business problem into a Six Sigma improvement project.

❑ Charter a team to conduct the analysis and implement the recommendations.

❑ Establish a schedule for project reviews and determine the resources required to perform the analysis.

❑ Gain the active participation of process owners and other significant stakeholders in the project's outcome.

❑ Define the business problem from a high-level perspective of its external customers.

❑ Determine what is critical to satisfaction for these customers.

❑ Provide input to the team to align the project to the original business problem.

A written project charter formally demonstrates that a project has the power of the organization and the support of its management team behind it. (For more details on the Define step, see Question 24.)

Measure

During this step, the Black Belt takes the lead to facilitate the project team through the following tasks:

❑ Identify characteristics of the product or process in question that are critical to customer satisfaction. These are the response variables (called Y's or output variables) that will be improved during the DMAIC process.

❑ Clarify how the process operates by developing a map of the activities involved and determining how the process can fail using a Failure Mode and Effects Analysis (FMEA).

❑ Evaluate which process factors are controllable—and, therefore, desirable aspects of a final solution.

❑ Define a performance standard for the delivery of products or services to customers and measure the current performance and available external benchmarks against this standard.

❑ Determine the cost of poor quality and establish a target for improvement.

❑ Validate the inherent capability of the measurement system to detect significant changes in process performance.

At the completion of the Measure step, a Black Belt should know the nature of the statistical problem (i.e., a need to shift the mean for the Y, reduce its variation, or both). (For more details on the Measure step, see Question 25.)

Analyze

The Black Belt performs most of the work during the Analyze step, sometimes with the support of a Green Belt and project-team members during data collection. This step involves the following tasks:

❑ Evaluate the current operation of the process in question to determine the potential sources of variation for critical performance parameters (called X's or independent variables).

❑ Link the sources of variation to control points in the process to provide "physical levers" for improvement once the analysis indicates how the process must be set for optimal performance results.

❑ Perform sequential "data mining" with statistical tools to identify factors that are sources of variation that have a significant impact on performance.

❑ Conduct a series of analyses. Begin with hypothesis testing to evaluate differences between factors. Move to analysis of variance to determine if samples come from the same population. Apply regression analysis to determine how much of the total variation is explained by the factors that have been identified.

At the completion of the Analyze step, the Black Belt, project champion, process owner, and Master Black Belt should all agree on improvement objectives based on the statistical process characterization. In addition, the path forward should be identified. (For more details on the Analyze step, see Question 26.)

Improve

During the Improve step, the solution to the problem is defined, and its effectiveness is demonstrated through a pilot experiment. The Black Belt leads the team through the following series of analytical steps.

❑ Screen potential sources of variation to determine their effects on shifting the process mean and on reducing the total process variation.

❑ Discover relationships and dependencies among the process variables by solving the business equation $y = f(x)$. Determine which factors (X's) drive process performance (Y).

❑ Determine, for the critical parameters of the process, the best operating characteristics (set points and tolerances) and the range over which optimal process performance can be maintained.

In addition to Six Sigma tools (e.g., design of experiments [DOE] and simulation analysis), the tools of lean management (e.g., setup-time reduction, cycle-time reduction, and value enhancement) are used during the Improve step. At the end of this step, the process owner should be convinced by the pilot demonstration that the recommended solution will resolve the defined business problem. (For more detail on the Improve step, see Question 27.)

Control

During the Control step, the solution to the problem is prepared for integration with the routine work process, and the support systems necessary for full-scale implementation are developed. Based on the recommended process changes, the work includes the following:

❑ Design and implement a statistically based control system (e.g., statistical process control, or SPC).

❑ Validate the measurement system to ensure it is capable of detecting and accurately reporting significant changes in process performance for the critical parameters.

❑ Calculate the process capability achieved by making the recommended changes.

❑ Develop a control plan to maintain the improved level of process performance.

❑ Implement the process controls on the revised process and train the operators to ensure their personal capability to interpret instructions and execute the process improvements.

This work is typically a joint effort of the Black Belt and the process owner, who work with the team that will use the new process. At the end of the Control step, this team should be able to manage its daily work using the improved process. (For more details on the Control step, see Question 28.)

Other facts about DMAIC

The DMAIC process formalizes the search for variables using the y = f (x) equation as an organizing method. It begins with investigation of the business Y's and then translates the results into meaningful process X's that can be managed by the organization.

Variation Discovery Process

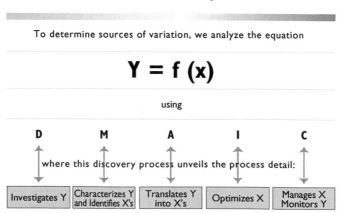

To determine sources of variation, we analyze the equation

$$Y = f (x)$$

using

D	M	A	I	C

where this discovery process unveils the process detail:

Investigates Y	Characterizes Y and Identifies X's	Translates Y into X's	Optimizes X	Manages X Monitors Y

Each of the five steps of the DMAIC process has a different objective. These objectives serve as decision filters in the search for the source of controllable variables and the control points that will maintain process performance in the desired operating range. The decision filters of the DMAIC process appear sequentially.

DMAIC Decision Filters

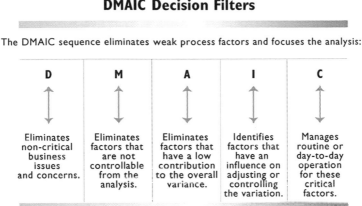

The DMAIC sequence eliminates weak process factors and focuses the analysis:

D	M	A	I	C
Eliminates non-critical business issues and concerns.	Eliminates factors that are not controllable from the analysis.	Eliminates factors that have a low contribution to the overall variance.	Identifies factors that have an influence on adjusting or controlling the variation.	Manages routine or day-to-day operation for these critical factors.

The realization review

The Control step is followed by an additional project activity called a *realization review*. This activity is an assessment of the financial benefits realized after a protracted implementation phase where the process owner makes recommended changes. The objective is to see if all the projected benefits of the project were realized and whether these benefits transferred to the bottom line.

In many organizations, this review is conducted by the finance or internal auditing department and can involve the Black Belt. This is also a good time to document the lessons learned from a project and extend all the observed benefits to similar business and work processes throughout the organization.

Lean-thinking and JIT tools

An additional set of improvement tools has recently been superimposed on the classic DMAIC statistical toolkit: the tools of lean thinking and just-in-time delivery (JIT). The diagram on the next page demonstrates how these tools integrate into each of the five steps of the DMAIC process. This approach works particularly well for business processes because the tools of lean thinking are appropriate for use by front-line workers, can be led by Green Belts, and require fairly uncomplicated (first-year algebra level) math skills.

Integrating Lean Thinking

Six Sigma integrates lean thinking to increase the efficiency of all business operations:

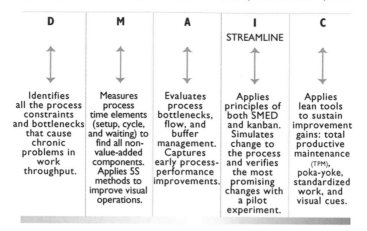

D	M	A	I STREAMLINE	C
Identifies all the process constraints and bottlenecks that cause chronic problems in work throughput.	Measures process time elements (setup, cycle, and waiting) to find all non-value-added components. Applies 5S methods to improve visual operations.	Evaluates process bottlenecks, flow, and buffer management. Captures early process-performance improvements.	Applies principles of both SMED and kanban. Simulates change to the process and verifies the most promising changes with a pilot experiment.	Applies lean tools to sustain improvement gains: total productive maintenance (TPM), poka-yoke, standardized work, and visual cues.

Specific details about how each DMAIC step operates and the role of business leaders in supporting Six Sigma projects are presented in Questions 24 through 28.

How does the Define step of DMAIC work?

Objectives

The five objectives of the Define step are to:

1. Specify the team charter.

2. Determine customer focus. This includes external, critical to satisfaction (CTS) and internal, critical to quality (CTQ) considerations.

3. Define the problem statement relative to the performance standard and observed level of achievement.

4. Plan the overall Six Sigma project.

5. Set improvement objectives for the project.

Definition

Define is the first step of the Six Sigma statistical problem-solving process. During this step, a problem is identified and quantified in terms of the customer-perceived result. The product and/or process to be improved is identified, resources for the improvement project are put in place, and expectations for the improvement project are set. The focus of the problem-solving strategy is kept on the customers' primary requirements.

During this step, the Black Belt works with his/her supervising Master Black Belt and sponsoring business leader to structure a project charter that identifies the problem statement, improvement objective, management target, project scope, project milestones, team members, and any special resources required to complete the project. Both the Master Black Belt and the sponsoring business leader should formally approve the charter, which provides the Black Belt with authority to conduct the analysis. This delegation of authority can help the Black Belt significantly if there are problems in getting data or conducting a pilot experiment. Because most problems occur between process boundaries, it is important that each involved process owner also ratify the project charter.

DMAIC analysis begins with the result of process performance (i.e., the business Y) and traces backward through the process steps to identify the operational factors that produced the result. Six Sigma projects should address the chronic problems of an organization, which most likely have cross-functional elements or are related to interactions among several variables. Since these problems use up a disproportionate amount of resources, it is important that they be solved as quickly as possible.

Inputs to the Define step

The figure below illustrates the inputs to the Define step. Inputs on the left side of the figure come from the prior Recognize step; those on the top describe concepts, principles, or methods used to facilitate the Define step; and those on the bottom identify the tools that are used. The outputs on the right lead to step two in the DMAIC process, the Measure step. The horizontal input/output flow in the figure indicates the linkage among the five DMAIC steps.

Thought Map for the Define Step

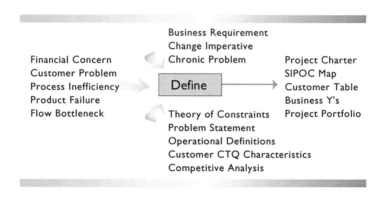

Initial meeting objectives

The project's sponsoring business leader should call an initial organizational meeting of all project participants: project champion, Master Black Belt, process owners, and technical experts. The purpose of this meeting is to accomplish the following objectives:

❯ Determine the scope of the problem.

❯ Understand the magnitude of the problem.

❯ Establish the importance of the problem.

❯ Define the problem and defect conditions using operational terms.

❯ Assign accountability for problem resolution and implementation.

❯ Determine who will participate on the team and their appropriate roles.

❯ Name a team leader.

Team charter

Draft a team charter that describes the symptoms of the problem and the context in which the business issue exists. (See Question 16 for details on drafting a project charter.)

- Describe the problem's impact on customers.
- Create operational definitions for the problem and the defects that must be resolved.
- Identify the major participants in the project and the role each must play in the resolution of the issue.
- Identify resources that will be dedicated to help resolve the problem. This includes process time for conducting tests and gathering data, as well as people who assist in analysis and data collection.

Questions to ask during the Define step

- Why was the project selected?
- What is the business problem?
- Have all affected business areas reviewed the project charter?
- How do we measure these business performance areas today?
- Why is this business area in need of improvement?
- How do we define a defect in performance for this area?
- Once we discover a defect, where do we observe it and when?
- How much is this problem costing the organization?
- Who are the customers, and what are their relevant requirements?
- What data has been collected to facilitate understanding of these requirements?
- What are the business reasons for completing this project?
- Are these business reasons compelling to the team?
- Has a similar project already been completed?
- What are the boundaries of this project?
- What is the goal for this project?
- How will we define success?
- Have the project milestones been set?
- How will the project benefit customers?
- How will the project benefit shareholders?

Define step deliverables

▶ The team understands the business outcome of the basic problem.

▶ The team understands the problem's apparent causes or symptoms.

▶ A high-level SIPOC process map has been created.

▶ The top few CTQ customer requirements for the product or process are balanced with strategic business requirements.

▶ A high-level process map graphically displays the major process events and potential set of business X's from management's viewpoint.

▶ A Black Belt is assigned to the project.

▶ The project charter is approved.

▶ The team charter describes the purpose and goals of the Six Sigma project and establishes the team's solution boundaries.

▶ Management conducts a project kick-off communication briefing for the team and all involved parties.

▶ The process owners are interested in the project, support its business objective, and encourage its completion.

▶ The work-process team members agree to cooperate with the project-analysis team and collaborate on the work required to accomplish the project objective.

Analysis tools

Techniques that support the investigations done during the Define step include the following:

▶ Project charter template

▶ SIPOC model

▶ Operational definitions

▶ Stakeholder analysis

▶ Kano model of customer satisfaction

▶ Customer surveys and market research

▶ Voice of the customer (VOC) analysis

▶ Customer-requirements analysis (CTS and CTQ tree)

▶ Enterprise map (business Y's)

▶ Business-process map (business X's)

▶ Throughput flow analysis and bottleneck identification

▶ Statistical process control (SPC) charts and run charts

▶ Sigma process baseline

- Basic graphical analysis methods
- Affinity Diagram
- Force-field analysis
- Root-cause analysis
- Cause & Effect/Fishbone Diagram
- Strategic benchmarking
- Risk-based decision making
- Road mapping
- Pareto chart

Define step activity checklist

- Develop an operational definition of the problem statement.
- Identify project scope and boundary conditions.
- Identify customers and CTQ characteristics.
- Develop a high-level SIPOC process map.
- Estimate customer satisfaction and cost of poor quality (COPQ).
- Evaluate historical baseline performance data for the process.
- Identify key process output variable (KPOV) metrics (i.e., process business Y's).
- Create project timeline.
- Update project-management system.

Define step summary

The objective of the Define step of DMAIC is to produce a project charter that clearly identifies the business problem that the Black Belt is commissioned to analyze. During this step, the project champion analyzes the problem's Y metrics to define critical issues requiring the Black Belt's high-level analytical skills. Successful completion of this step results in a focused project where the level of analysis required is appropriate for a Six Sigma investigation and non-critical business issues are eliminated. The project champion (who might also be the process owner) and the Master Black Belt perform much of the work during the Define step.

How does the Measure step of DMAIC work?

Objectives

Identify the current process capability of the business system in question, as well as its process-performance baseline and measurement-system capability, and determine important contributing factors to the variation observed.

Definition

The Measure step enables an organization to understand the present condition of its work processes before it attempts to identify where they can be improved. The Measure step provides the substance for the problem statement. During this step, the critical-to-quality characteristics, or CTQs (Y and y), are defined, as well as the defects in the process or product in question, and the measurement of the y is validated. During this step, a physical model of the process is developed through a graphical analysis. Black Belts scrutinize the process to see what happens as input is transitioned to output. They also create a logical model of the process (using the interrelationships among the measurement elements) to gain a linked, quantitative understanding of the process-performance relationships. All the factors that influence the output are evaluated, and potential effects they have on failure modes are identified. The Measure step is based on valid data, so it eliminates guesswork about how well a process is working.

During the Measure step, the Black Belt leads the team in learning about the operation of the business process in question. The team maps the process for flow, feedback loops, measurement-control points, and hand-offs across organizational groups. The team then works to identify the logical structure of the problem by analyzing the system of performance measures using y = f (x). When the logical link is made between performance measures and the measures critical to customer satisfaction (CTS), the team focuses on the controllable factors they discover in their analysis of the process-failure opportunities.

The Black Belt also leads the team through a study to find out how much sensitivity the measurement system has to detect a change that is meaningful to customers. The team can improve the measurement system to ensure it is valid and then begin collecting process-performance data to set the performance baseline for the process. The baseline is the set of indicators that defines a starting point for improvement of the process.

Once the current performance is understood, the Black Belt can conduct a process-capability study to determine how good the process can become without any capital investment or major changes. The gap between this and the current performance is the improvement opportunity requested in the Six Sigma project charter. Once this is known, a financial estimate can be made of the cost created by this performance gap.

Inputs to the Measure step

The figure below illustrates the inputs to the Measure step. Inputs on the left side of the figure come from the prior Define step; those on the top describe concepts, principles, or methods used to facilitate the Measure step; and those on the bottom identify the tools that are used. The outputs on the right lead to step three in the DMAIC process, the Analyze step. The horizontal input/output flow in the figure indicates the linkage among the five DMAIC steps.

Thought Map for the Measure step

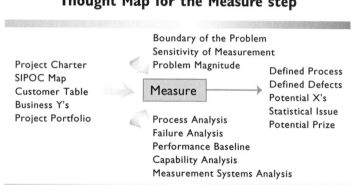

Questions to ask during the Measure step

▶ What is the operational definition of the problem?

▶ What are the potential defects, and how are they operationally defined?

▶ What impact does the Y measure have on our business?

▶ Does our measurement system for Y detect important shifts?

▶ What is our performance baseline?

▶ What is the statistical problem?

▶ Are we delivering what the customer wants?

▶ How good is our measurement system?

▶ What is our real performance today?

- How good could our performance possibly be?
- What is the gap between these two performance levels?
- What is the cost of this poor quality?
- Where is the process operating ineffectively?
- Where is the process dissatisfying customers?
- Where can the process fail? How can it fail? What are the results of these potential failures? How is the customer affected by these failures?
- How do we know we are attacking the right problem?
- What do we need to focus on to resolve the problem?
- What input, process, and output measures are involved in the performance of this process?
- Does the process diagram reflect reality?
- Is there consensus about the problem definition?
- Does the measurement validation stand up?
- Were changes made to the current measurement system that will allow a clearer identification of the problem? Were these changes validated by a measurement-systems analysis?
- Were those changes captured?
- Did the number of defects per million opportunities (DPMO) change dramatically?

Measure step deliverables

- Clearly defined process-output measures (Y's)
- A measurable and defined performance standard
- An accurate assessment of the current process performance
- Valid data on the customer CTQs (Y's) and output variables (y's)
- Corrected deficiencies in the measurement system
- Real-world model of the process
- Knowledge of the potential causes of the problem
- Knowledge of controllable factors in the process
- Knowledge of the sensitivity of our measurement system
- Estimation of potential process performance
- Documentation of actual process performance
- Identification of productivity loss

- Calculation of the cost of poor quality (COPQ)
- Process-performance baseline

Analysis tools

The following techniques support the investigations done during the Measure step.

- Deployment diagrams
- Critical-to-tree analysis for transition of CTSes to CTQs
- Customer-satisfaction survey
- Thought map
- Cause & Effect/Fishbone Diagram
- Failure Mode and Effects Analysis (FMEA)
- Severity and failure criticality analysis
- Fault tree analysis (FTA)
- $y = f(x)$ analysis and MECE analysis
- Process-capability analysis
- Descriptive statistics
- Basic graphical analysis
- Process benchmarking
- Measurement systems analysis (MSA)/capability study
- Baseline performance determination
- Statistical process control (SPC) charts and run charts
- Rolled throughput yield (RTY)
- Financial analysis and COPQ estimation
- Team charter, problem statement, and operational definition
- Box diagram (multi-vari analysis chart)

Tasks in which the Black Belt leads the team

- Create a statistical problem definition (to shift the mean or reduce variation).
- Determine the current state of performance.
- Evaluate the process capability.
- Calculate the cost of poor quality.
- Analyze performance in terms of customer satisfaction.
- Determine process-failure opportunities.

- Ensure connection of measures to CTS factors.
- Assess measurement-system capability.
- Determine significant performance factors.
- Revise the team charter as required.

What is known at this step's completion?

- The full definition of the practical problem.
- How the process really operates.
- Some factors that influence outcomes.
- Some factors that do not influence outcomes.
- How the process can fail and why.
- What is important to the customers.
- Whether the data is good enough to continue.

Measure step activity checklist

- Define the key process input variables (KPIVs, or X's).
- Determine $y = f(x)$.
- Prepare a deployment diagram of the process.
- Develop a data-collection plan and analysis approach.
- Analyze and validate the measurement system and collect performance data.
- Establish the baseline DPMO/sigma level.
- Refine the project objective and the scope of the project.
- Update the project-management system.

Measure step summary

The objective of the Measure step of DMAIC is to characterize Y factors and establish the basis for hypotheses about a problem. Hypotheses about a problem's cause must take real-world considerations into account to determine the contribution that each controllable factor makes to the total variation observed in the problem.

The work performed during the Measure step focuses on the characterization of the problem. This includes describing the relevant business and work processes; identifying the measurements and their relationships; linking the process measures to customer concerns; determining which measures are controllable and can be considered part of the potential solution set; analyzing the measurement system to ensure it is sensitive enough to detect change that is meaningful to customers; understanding the potential failure modes and their effect on the process as well as their severity for outcomes; and synthesizing the learning from this step to prepare for detailed data analysis. Work performed during the Measure step is performed by the Black Belt, process owner, and process team and is monitored by a Master Black Belt.

How does the Analyze step of DMAIC work?

Objectives

Analyze process-performance data to localize sources of controllable variation, determine the root cause of the problem, and determine areas to address as opportunities for improving the process.

Definition

The Analyze step adds statistical strength to problem analysis. Statistical analysis identifies a problem's root cause by determining which factors contribute to the observed variation and how much of the total variation is explained by these factors. Statistical tools can be used to calculate how much variation each dominant factor contributes to the overall problem. Hypothesis testing is used to establish which factors make a difference in process performance and identify relationships among the X factors. A Pareto chart of contributions can be used to prioritize the investigation. Interaction effects among the process variables can be observed through statistical testing.

When the analysis is complete, the dominant sources of controllable variation are identified. This helps in identifying the area on which to focus when building a final solution during the Improve step.

Oh, no! Theory O!

Theory O is a style of management in which all decisions are based on opinion rather than validated by facts. Many analysis tools, such as brainstorming and Affinity Diagrams, support such a subjective approach to decision making because they are based on the ideas of groups of people (sometimes called organizational wisdom). Often such wisdom can lead to "commonsense" solutions to problems.

When these solutions fail to produce results that resolve a problem, it is time to develop hypotheses and test them with statistical tools to find the root cause and produce a fact-based solution. A big benefit of Six Sigma is the resolution of chronic problems.

Inputs to the Analyze step

The figure below illustrates the inputs to the Analyze step. Inputs on the left side of the figure come from the prior Measure step; those on the top describe concepts, principles, or methods used to facilitate the Analyze step; and those on the bottom identify the tools that are used. The outputs on the right lead to step four in the DMAIC process, the Improve step. The horizontal input/output flow in the figure indicates the linkage among the five DMAIC steps.

Thought Map for the Analyze Step

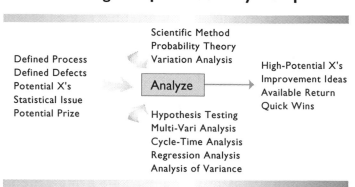

Questions to ask during the Analyze step

▶ What data should we collect?

▶ How good are our measurements?

▶ How much data is needed?

▶ Do the means of samples come from the same underlying population?

▶ What relationships exist in the data?

▶ What sources of variation can be identified?

▶ Which of these sources represent key factors in successfully controlling the output of the process?

▶ What evidence is available to suggest that a particular factor is both statistically and practically significant?

▶ If we used tools that require normality, have we tested the data for normality?

▶ Does the project use a logical method that is easily understood?

▶ Has the analysis answered the questions in the charter?

▶ What process changes are needed for us to improve?

▶ How will we know that we have improved?

- How will we know if the improvement objectives are met?
- What savings are possible with this improvement?
- How can we demonstrate the solution's effectiveness?

Analyze step deliverables

- Determination of which variables shift the mean or reduce variation
- Determination of which variables shift the mean and reduce variation
- Determination of which variables are not important

Analysis tools

Techniques that support the investigations done during the Analyze step include the following:

- Basic quality tools
- Normal probability plot and test for normality
- Rational sub-grouping
- Cycle-time analysis
- Bottleneck analysis
- Hypothesis formulation
- Confidence intervals
- Statistical sampling
- Statistical tests of difference
- Multi-vari analysis
- Correlation analysis
- Time-series analysis
- Cross-tabulations and tally analysis
- Contingency table analysis
- Chi-squared goodness of fit
- General linear model
- Analysis of variance
- Analysis of means
- Analysis of covariance
- Regression analysis, general linear model, residuals analysis, and R^2 statistic
- Logistic regression analysis

- Process-capability analysis
- Analysis of variation
- Regression analysis

Analyze step activity checklist

- Complete thought-process maps.
- Benchmark process performance for key process output variables (KPOVs) (i.e., business Y's).
- Determine sources of variance for business Y's, based on regression-analysis test for completeness of the set of variables.
- Quantify key process input variables (KPIVs) and improvement opportunities.
- Perform root-cause analysis.
- Define performance-improvement targets.
- Obtain process-owner approval.
- Update project-management system.

Analyze step summary

The objective of the Analyze step of DMAIC is to use data from the Measure step to localize and evaluate sources of controllable variation and determine their root causes. The work performed during this step is highly statistical and done primarily by the Black Belt. This work includes evaluating performance differences among factors to establish and test hypotheses against real-world data; determining how much each factor contributes to the total observed variation; identifying the influence of factors (X's) on response (Y) mean and variance; identifying interactions among process variables; determining if all principal factors have been analyzed; calculating the process-performance baseline; and defining the cost of poor quality. The team supports the Black Belt through data collection and interpretation. The Master Black Belt reviews the use of analytical tools. The project champion and process owner review and interpret the analysis to ensure it meets the business objective.

▶ TIP

The first three steps of the DMAIC process (Define, Measure, and Analyze) characterize the nature of the problem to be solved. Upon completion of these steps, the problem and its root cause(s) are known and the project charter becomes a finalized document. One way to use Six Sigma's analytical tools to attack a broadly scoped problem is to analyze it through characterization to identify a number of related projects. A Black Belt can work on these projects in a well-coordinated manner under the supervision of a Master Black Belt.

How does the Improve step of DMAIC work?

Objectives

The three objectives of the Improve step are to:

1. Experiment with the process to improve its performance.

2. Determine set points for process optimization.

3. Design and conduct pilot tests that confirm the operation of the most promising improvement opportunities.

Definition

The Improve step focuses on the previously agreed-upon opportunity for business improvement. The work performed during this step is statistical and done primarily by the Black Belt. This work includes identifying the process factors that statistically solve the problem by shifting the mean or reducing the variance (or both); demonstrating the ability to control a process by setting the level of these parameters; validating optimal set points for continuously operating the process; and developing an implementation solution that ensures sustainable and predictable performance in the face of identified failure opportunities.

During this step, team members support the Black Belt by performing data collection and interpretation during experiments. The Master Black Belt reviews the experimental process plan and its application. Management endorses the findings. The project champion or process owner gives the Black Belt financial and practical support (e.g., screening, optimization, and validation) for conducting experiments and performs regular project reviews to interpret analysis results.

Inputs to the Improve step

The figure on the next page illustrates the inputs to the Improve step. Inputs on the left side of the figure come from the prior Analyze step; those on the top describe concepts, principles, or methods used to facilitate the Improve step; and those on the bottom identify the tools that are used. The outputs on the right lead to step five in the DMAIC process, the Control step. The horizontal input/output flow in the figure indicates the linkage among the five DMAIC steps.

Thought Map for the Improve Step

High-Potential X's
Improvement Ideas
Available Return
Quick Wins

Experimental Design
Variables Sorting
Sequential Search

Improve

Shainin Methods
Taguchi Techniques
Simulation Analysis
Design of Experiments (DOE)
Tolerance Analysis

Mean Shifters
Variation Managers
Pilot Results
Budget Request

Questions to ask during the Improve step

▶ What is the practical significance of the key X's identified during the Analyze step?

▶ How do we control, block, or design out the vital few X's?

▶ Which of the potential solutions makes the most sense so far?

▶ How does each potential solution address the root cause of the problem?

▶ What assumptions underlie each potential solution? Are they valid?

▶ How will each of these potential solutions impact the people involved with the process? What preparation will they need so their work will go smoothly after the change is made?

▶ Which sources of variation contribute the most to the overall variation in the Y's?

▶ Which key factors contribute the most to managing the location of the Y average?

▶ Which of the key factors contribute the most to reducing variation in the Y?

▶ If an experiment is required, how large should it be?

▶ Does the measurement system need to be changed before conducting this pilot experiment?

▶ How will we control the critical parameters?

▶ How should tolerance limits be set to ensure the parameter levels are robust in the face of uncontrolled variables?

▶ How well does the confirmation run of the pilot experiment reflect the value of the recommended improvements?

▶ Do the analysis residuals suggest further improvement opportunities?

▶ What benefits can be projected from this pilot for full-scale implementation?

▶ What major milestones are required for a successful implementation plan?

▶ What are the potential problems with this plan?

▶ What countermeasures have we considered for these potential problem areas?

- What mistake-proofing can be done to eliminate these potential problem areas?
- Who must be involved in the Control step to ensure acceptance of the solution?

Improve step deliverables

- Key X's that will deliver the desired performance in Y.
- Operating envelope for these X's that consistently delivers the targeted Y value.
- Tolerance limits for setting these X's to maintain a robust output of the Y target.
- Practical observations for maintaining control of the X's that are based on the pilot experiment and demonstrate the potential to achieve the desired results.
- Budget estimate to fund the desired change.

Analysis tools

The following techniques support the investigations done during the Improve step.

- Shainin statistical reasoning
- Multi-vari analysis
- Design of experiments (DOE)
- Discrete event simulation
- Full factorial DOE
- Fractional factorial DOE
- Mixture experimental designs
- Blocking experimental designs
- Inferential statistics
- Taguchi analysis
- Placket-Burman experimental designs
- Box-Behnken experimental designs
- Central composite experimental designs (CCD)
- Response surface method (RSM)
- Moving averages
- Auto-regressive moving averages (ARIMA)
- Exponentially weighted moving averages (EWMA)
- Cumulative sum (CuSum) control charts
- Evolutionary operation (EVOP)
- Statistical tolerance analysis
- The lean-enterprise 5S housekeeping system

Tasks in which the Black Belt leads the team

▶ Design an experiment (or conduct a simulation) to demonstrate the effect of high-potential X's on the performance of Y.

▶ Analyze the results of the experiment.

▶ Conduct statistical tolerance analysis of the key parameters to determine the best operating set points for each.

▶ Identify mistake-proofing opportunities for all key operator-controllable factors.

▶ Conduct a final estimate of the project's benefit potential.

What is known at this step's completion?

▶ A statistical definition of the practical problem (a need to shift the mean or reduce the variation).

▶ An acceptable solution that is ready for implementation.

▶ The workers who will be affected by the changes and require revised documentation.

Improve step activity checklist

▶ Diagnose key process input variable (KPIV) performance and goals.

▶ Identify solution options.

▶ Determine and implement an optimal solution.

▶ Update the process Failure Mode and Effects Analysis (FMEA).

▶ Do the final cost/benefit analysis and implementation budget.

▶ Develop a project-improvement plan based on the experiment results.

▶ Validate process improvements in the pilot.

▶ Update the project-management system.

Improve step summary

The objective of the Improve step of DMAIC is to identify factors that control the statistical problem, shift the critical factors' mean to the target performance, and/or reduce the amount of variation to make the process perform consistently within the limits desired by customers. Robust performance is obtained by controlling the critical factors in a way that ensures the standard of performance is consistently delivered.

The pilot experiment validates the factors that affect process performance. It helps management understand the risk dimensions of a full-scale implementation and ensures worker agreement with the change because workers first observe the performance improvement on a smaller scale. A pilot experiment sometimes uncovers unanticipated problems that can be corrected before the solution is completely implemented.

How does the Control step of DMAIC work?

Objectives

The objective of the Control step is to produce a project-control plan that does the following:

1. Delivers sustained optimal performance.

2. Disseminates improvement results across the entire organization.

3. Institutionalizes the improvements so they become part of the daily work routine.

4. Institutes a performance-monitoring system to ensure corrective action is taken if the process deviates from its design parameters.

The Control step also ensures consistency in the application of the knowledge gained in other areas of the organization that can benefit from it.

Definition

The work performed during the Control step primarily affects the process owner and implementation team. The work of the Black Belt facilitates the definition of an action plan to meet improvement-project objectives. The Black Belt's actions during this step include determining practical conditions that ensure the "solution space" is maintained; identifying training needs of front-line workers to ensure that process-performance consistency is achieved at all levels and across all shifts; mistake-proofing the process to ensure that minor errors do not reduce process performance; preparing statistical controls to keep the performance of critical process factors optimal; and translating statistical concepts into common language to ensure front-line acceptance.

Inputs to the Control step

The figure on the next page illustrates the inputs to the Control step. Inputs on the left side of the figure come from the prior Improve step; those on the top describe concepts, principles, or methods used to facilitate the Control step; and those on the bottom identify the tools that are used. The outputs on the right lead to the implementation of the recommended process improvements. The horizontal input/output flow in the figure indicates the linkage among the five DMAIC steps.

Thought Map for the Control Step

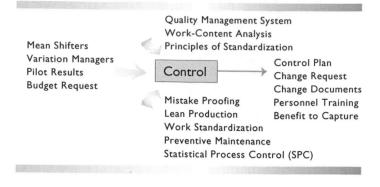

Mean Shifters
Variation Managers
Pilot Results
Budget Request

Quality Management System
Work-Content Analysis
Principles of Standardization

Control

Control Plan
Change Request
Change Documents
Personnel Training
Benefit to Capture

Mistake Proofing
Lean Production
Work Standardization
Preventive Maintenance
Statistical Process Control (SPC)

Questions to ask during the Control step

▶ How can we ensure the problem will not recur?

▶ Are the learnings from this project transferable to other areas of the organization?

▶ Does the final report comprehensively document all project work?
Check for the following:

  – New procedures and policies are documented as approved standards and included in the notebook.

  – Data analyses are presented so other Black Belts can replicate them.

  – To what degree have the final benefits been captured? What remains to be done to capture the remaining benefits?

▶ Have we provided for appropriate recognition and celebration for the team?

Control step deliverables

▶ Determine the practical set of conditions that must exist to ensure the "solution space" is maintained.

▶ Identify the training needs of workers to ensure that consistency can be achieved for all workers involved in process operations.

▶ Mistake-proof the process to ensure that minor errors cannot reduce process performance.

▶ Prepare a statistical control mechanism to sustain the performance of the change factors in the demonstrated optimal range.

▶ Translate the statistical mechanisms into the language of the workplace to ensure front-line understanding.

▶ Document the process changes in standard operating procedures and work instructions.

- Implement validated measurement systems to alert workers to changes in process conditions.
- Train all workers about revisions to routine work procedures and evaluate their comprehension of the new way of working.
- Integrate process changes into management review checklists and all routine process-performance-measurement reporting systems.
- Post process-performance trends to ensure visibility of the critical performance factors within the workplace.
- Identify all areas within the business where similar types of operations occur.
- Present the analysis findings and results of performance improvement to their process owners.
- Challenge these process owners to incorporate the lessons learned into their business areas.
- Provide consulting support from the Black Belt during the application to these other business areas.
- Measure all similar processes using the established critical success factors to demonstrate the achieved improvement in capability.
- Schedule a realization review to determine and document total project-related savings.

Analysis tools

Techniques that support the investigations done during the Control step include the following:

- Control plan
- Pre-control
- Positrol log
- Process housekeeping (5S)
- Visual factory
- Work balancing
- ISO 9000
- Standard operating procedures
- Long-term measurement capability study
- Statistical process control (SPC) charts
- Preventive maintenance
- Reliability-centered maintenance
- Business-controls audit

Task in which the Black Belt leads the team

▶ Develop the control plan, operating documentation, training aids, and statistical tools needed to implement the recommended change identified during the Improve step.

What is known at this step's completion?

▶ The disciplined work required to ensure consistency in process output at the targeted level of performance.

▶ A mistake-proof environment has been developed to assure management that the system is in a state of statistical control.

Control step activity checklist

▶ Mistake-proof the plan.

▶ Develop controls (SPCs) for KPIV metrics.

▶ Develop monitoring plan for KPOV metrics.

▶ Develop long-term measurement systems analysis (MSA) monitoring plan.

▶ Establish or update standard procedures.

▶ Update training.

▶ Validate process controls with process owner.

▶ Establish audit plan.

▶ Prepare the project's final report and lessons learned.

▶ Obtain process-owner approval for management change.

Control step summary

The objective of the Control step of DMAIC is to design and implement a change to effect improvements based on the results demonstrated during the Improve step. The human element of the process is engaged to implement and manage changes in daily work activities required to achieve the targeted result of the change project. The Control step also involves monitoring the process to ensure it has the discipline required to implement the change, capture the estimated improvement benefits, and maintain performance gains over the long term.

What happens during
Six Sigma project reviews?

Many organizations translate the steps of DMAIC and DMADV into tollgate or milestone reviews. This approach adds an extra element of discipline to Black Belt projects. These reviews, which are conducted to evaluate a project's business and technical elements, are performed by the Master Black Belt and project champion. In addition, the senior management team can elect to hold reviews at the end of the Define, Analyze, and Control steps to ensure the project contributes to the organization's strategic direction. Finally, to ensure projected benefits are realized and budgets reflect financial improvements, the project's sponsors conduct a realization review. (See Question 32 for a discussion about the role of a finance organization in this milestone review process.)

Throughout a Six Sigma project, management conducts at least six milestone reviews to determine the progress being made on the project and the effectiveness of the work accomplished. Three are simultaneous business and project reviews that can be jointly held with the project team (made up of the process owners, project champions, and Master Black Belt) and the senior management team. (These occur at the end of the Analyze and Control DMAIC steps and during the realization review.) Of the other three reviews, one covering the initiation and agenda signing is conducted by the project sponsor at the end of the Define step. The other two are conducted by the process owners, project champion, and Master Black Belt at the end of the Measure and Improve DMAIC steps.

All project reviews feature a fixed agenda, which consists of a set of questions asked by the project champion and the Black Belt, to ensure that progress is being made in applying the Six Sigma methodology. The set of questions asked by project champions keeps the focus on business issues. The Master Black Belt conducts a technical review to ensure that all statistical and graphical methods are used in an appropriate manner. Each review focuses on an analytical process performed during a particular step of the DMAIC process: project definition (Define), process measurement (Measure), factor analysis (Analyze), pilot experiment improvement (Improve), and process control (Control).

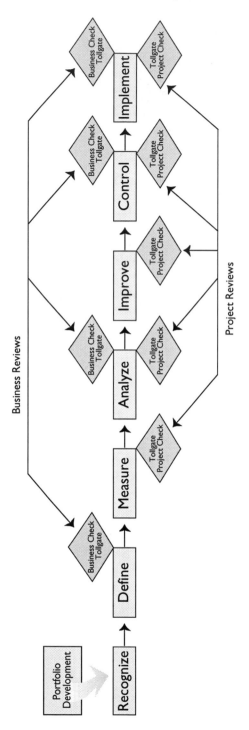

The realization review includes an audit that ensures the projected savings have occurred and the improvements have been fully implemented. Project champions work with the process owners who carry out the project recommendations to ensure that financial benefits are captured and implementation of the recommendations is done in a timely manner. The project champion normally asks a local financial manager to conduct the realization review to ensure an independent estimate of savings is done. Financial benefits are realized when funds are eliminated from a budget and the project's cost is recovered from the benefits.

How should a Six Sigma project review be conducted?

Project completion in a Six Sigma program is driven by a sequence of reviews that encourage the Black Belt to make progress. The most important aspect of this review process is the questions used to guide the Black Belt through the DMAIC process. These questions come from the perspective of either the business leader, who is charged with ensuring that the project culminates in appropriate commercial results, or the Master Black Belt, who is responsible for ensuring that the Black Belt properly meets the technical requirements of the project analysis.

The questions used to stimulate progress for each step of the DMAIC process are listed below. They are presented from the perspective of both the business leader and the Master Black Belt.

Define step review questions

▶ **Business leader**

1. What are the symptoms of the problem?

2. In what business process and operational context does this issue exist?

3. What is the defect from our customers' perspective? Under what conditions does it occur?

4. What is the impact of the problem on our customers? How does it affect their ability to use our product or service?

5. How have you operationally defined the problem and the related defect from the perspective of our customers? How have you translated the customer problem into a process problem and focused the team on an issue that is resolvable?

6. How does this project relate to our strategic business assumptions?

7. Does the project have an appropriate scope? Should a Master Black Belt more fully characterize the problem before it is defined as a Black Belt–level project?

8. What resources are needed to properly resolve this problem?

9. Who are the most appropriate team members to work on this problem? What roles should they assume?

10. What help do you need?

▶ Master Black Belt

1. What is the business issue to be attacked?

2. Why was this project selected over competing projects?

3. What are the symptoms of the problem as perceived by management?

4. How have you quantified this problem as a business Y?

5. How do our business priorities align with this project?

6. Has a similar project been done before, and if so, what was learned?

7. What is your study plan to initiate the project?

Measure step review questions

▶ Business leader

1. How well does the process flow? Where are the restrictions and "hidden factories" that reduce productivity?

2. How good is the measurement system? Does it detect output changes that are significant to our customers? Does it add bias that adversely influences the interpretation of the observations?

3. What level of process performance have we achieved? Where has our process performance declined?

4. What quick wins are achievable to improve performance or capture savings?

5. What are the most probable forms of potential failure? Have we mistake-proofed this process for these failure modes?

6. How well does this process perform compared to key external benchmarks of performance for similar work processes? How does it compare with similar internal work processes?

7. Does the project team have sufficient resources to continue its work on this project?

▶ Master Black Belt

1. How has the business objective become refined as a result of your preliminary baseline analysis?

2. How is this business problem logically related to our external customers using the $y = f(x)$ MECE logic?

3. What can you observe about the nature of the problem in the physical world?

4. How is the observed, real-world problem reflected in the logical world of work measurements (comparing graphical and statistical analysis methods)?

5. Is the business data-collection system capable of producing precise, accurate, and timely information? If not, what corrections can be made to improve it?

6. What lessons have been learned in this initial analysis of the project?

7. What rapid improvements can be implemented as a result of learning from the Measure step?

Analyze step review questions

▶ **Business leader**

1. Which measurement factors most strongly influence business performance?

2. Which X factors contribute the most to cost of poor quality and non-value-added cycle time? Where do process-quality losses and non-value-adding tasks occur?

3. Where do bottlenecks exist that inhibit productivity? How well do your theories about productivity loss work out when tested with performance data?

4. How much process variation can be explained by the analysis of the process performance? Do the sources of variation account for all performance losses?

5. How consistent is observed performance across all similar operations?

6. What rapid improvements can be implemented as a result of learning from the Analyze step?

7. What is the estimate of the potential cost savings from this project?

▶ **Master Black Belt**

1. Where are the critical parameters measured in the system?

2. What is the key measurement at each critical physical control point?

3. Have the precision and accuracy of the current measurements been established?

4. What factors contribute to the variation of this measure?

5. How much variation in the key business Y has been explained?

6. Is there evidence of missing variables based on examination of the residuals? Does the R-square statistic indicate the problem has been well defined?

7. Does the project team have sufficient resources to continue its work?

Improve step review questions

▶ **Business leader**

1. What are best settings for operating this process at minimum cost and maximum effectiveness?

2. How sensitive is this work-process operation to changes in critical performance factors?

3. Does this work in practice as well as it does in theory?

4. How much can the revised process drift before the customer will perceive a difference in the process output?

5. What tolerance band should be established around the process set points?

6. Will your change recommendations be easy to implement?

7. Does the project team have sufficient resources to conduct the demonstration test?

❯ Master Black Belt

1. What process areas need to be improved? How does the data point to specific opportunities?

2. Which performance measures are the most critical to operations?

3. What is the operating envelope for controlling critical parameters?

4. How should tolerance limits be set to ensure these parameter levels are robust in the face of uncontrolled variables?

5. How well does the confirmation (or pilot run) reflect the value of the improvements recommended?

6. Do the analysis residuals suggest further improvement opportunities?

7. What lessons have been learned from the work done during the Improve step?

Control step review questions

❯ Business leader

1. What are practical changes that must accompany the process change for it to be accepted in the workplace?

2. How have the statistical analyses been translated into work that must be done by front-line employees?

3. How will the control mechanisms sustain the performance of the process as it goes through natural shifts in variation?

4. Will all potential concerns with this process be eliminated before it is released to operators for full-scale implementation?

5. What is the final estimate of potential savings? On what schedule will these savings be captured?

6. Who is responsible for monitoring and managing this revised process? When will they next report on its performance?

7. Do you have the full cooperation of all team members for implementation?

❯ Master Black Belt

1. What are the critical control factors? How are they currently controlled in the workplace?

2. What skills are required to control these factors? How will front-line workers gain these skills and keep them honed over time?

3. How will work processes be protected from errors and mistakes?

4. What changes must be made in training programs and work instructions before the business-control system can be effectively managed?

5. If capital funds were available, would the improvement choice change?

6. How can the lessons learned during this project be applied in other areas of the company?

7. Do the process owners in these areas have adequate resources to implement the recommendations?

Realization review questions

▶ **Business leader**

1. Have workers been given an opportunity to critique and revise all changes to their work environment in an effort to convince them of the true value of the proposed change?

2. Have all work procedures been changed to reflect revised process-operation requirements?

3. Have all employees been trained in the new methods?

4. Have all employees been tested to demonstrate they have learned and mastered the changes to their work procedures?

5. Have job descriptions and competence requirements been aligned to the new job requirements?

6. Have job aids been developed to mistake-proof the procedures that have changed?

7. Can these improvements be used elsewhere in the organization?

▶ **Master Black Belt**

1. Does the process owner need anything else to ensure smooth implementation?

2. At what phase should the process be re-evaluated to ensure the improvements have been implemented correctly?

3. Where can the lessons of this project be applied to other process areas to achieve further business improvements?

4. What analysis methods have proven most useful? Are there any lessons that

should be shared with other Black Belts?

5. How have you communicated the results of this project to other Black Belts and the rest of the company?

6. Have you completed a project storyboard to summarize this report?

7. When will the final report be complete and the project ready for sign-off?

What does a Master Black Belt do?

Master Black Belts are internal technical consultants who train, coach, and mentor an organization's Black Belts in the use of Six Sigma tools. They also help Black Belts get through difficult parts of their analysis during Six Sigma projects. In addition, Master Black Belts perform the following tasks:

▶ Coordinate large projects that span across an organization's functional and process areas.

▶ Assist business leaders and process owners in defining projects.

▶ Provide routine technical milestone reviews for Black Belt projects.

▶ Conduct one or two DMAIC projects annually in areas of particular strategic interest.

▶ Help management build an analytical business model.

▶ Develop enterprise measurement systems to diagnose the performance of balanced-scorecard measures that support organizational performance priorities, such as shareholder value and brand value.

▶ Serve as an organization's measurement owner for implementation of its Six Sigma customer dashboard or balanced scorecard (see Question 44).

▶ Help to build the infrastructure of Six Sigma by doing tasks such as database capturing of analytical reports, holding meetings to develop Black Belts, and sponsoring internal conferences for spotlighting project results.

Master Black Belt position description

▶ **Management Activities**

❏ Assist an assigned business area's leadership team in developing an enterprise model and measurement map for managing operations.

❏ Act as a coach and advisor for defining a portfolio of Six Sigma projects for a business area.

❏ Assist the management team in identification of Six Sigma projects that encourage the completion of strategic business objectives.

- Develop and maintain the project-management infrastructure for Six Sigma projects in an assigned business area.
- Identify suitable candidates for Black Belt training and recommend them to business leaders and project champions.

▶ Technical Activities

- Instruct training and workshops for project champions, Black Belts, and Green Belts.
- Coach and advise Black Belts during projects to ensure that statistical tools are correctly used, results are interpreted properly, the DMAIC process is managed correctly, and that, where appropriate, new tools are applied in situations beyond the scope of the basic Black Belt training.
- Provide technical direction for all Six Sigma projects conducted within a specific business or operating area.
- Facilitate major cross-functional Six Sigma DMAIC and DMADV projects.

Master Black Belt selection criteria

- All candidates must complete training and certification as a Black Belt (i.e., basic training program, training project, and independent qualification project).
- It is desirable for candidates to have completed at least five Black Belt projects.
- Business knowledge is required. Candidates should possess technical astuteness in either business/commercial or technical/engineering applications. Role-model behavior in alignment with the organization's culture is required.
- Good interpersonal communication, facilitation, and coaching skills are needed for working across the functional boundaries and reporting levels of the organization.
- Experience in instruction is desirable, but not required.
- Expertise in a specific analytical tool or application of Six Sigma is desirable.

Master Black Belt development plan

The development program for Master Black Belts begins with the initial screening of Black Belt candidates during their certification training and continues through the execution of candidates' first two projects (i.e., the training project and initial independent project). This screening is based on on-the-job performance and results in a recommendation for consideration as a Master Black Belt.

To obtain a recommendation, each candidate must demonstrate to his/her business-area leaders that he/she possesses the necessary skills, aptitude, and knowledge required to be a Master Black Belt. Each candidate must also demonstrate a strong competence in both the technical skills of Six Sigma and the interpersonal skills of coaching, teaching, facilitating, consulting, and mentoring.

Once a candidate has passed this screening, the management team must determine if this career move is aligned with his/her long-term career interest and whether the person can be transitioned to the position at this time. Following selection, a candidate is enrolled in Master Black Belt training. This two-week program prepares candidates for the experience of becoming a Master Black Belt.

Upon successful completion of the Master Black Belt development program, in very large organizations a candidate can emphasize one of two career-specialty pathways:

❑ **Master Black Belt instructor:** This specialty focuses on instruction of Black Belt and Green Belt training courses.

❑ **Master Black Belt project manager:** This specialty focuses on managing large cross-functional DMADV projects for either business-process reengineering or new product development.

Master Black Belt training program

Below is the agenda for a typical two-week training program. These two weeks are separated by a one-month interval.

Week 1: Instructional-skills development

❑ Professional development of a Master Black Belt

❑ Teaching the DMAIC Define and Measure steps

❑ Teaching the DMAIC Analyze step

❑ Teaching the DMAIC Improve step

❑ Teaching the DMAIC Control step

❑ Design for Six Sigma (DFSS) project management and scorecards

❑ Master Black Belt case-study specification

Week 2: Project-management development

❑ Homework and case-study review

❑ Conducting Black Belt DMAIC project reviews

❑ DMAIC analysis tools:

  – Analytical Hierarchy Process (AHP)

  – Contingency tables

  – Logistic regression

  – Time-series analysis

  – Moving averages (EWMA and ARIMA)

- Cumulative sum (CuSum) control charts
- Evolutionary operation (EVOP)
- Shainin variables search technique
- General linear model
- Taguchi analysis
- Complex design of experiments (DOE)
- Response surface method (RSM)

❑ DMADV analysis tools:
- Quality function deployment (QFD)
- Pugh matrix
- Function Analysis System Technique (FAST)
- TRIZ approach to problem solving
- Reliability growth management

❑ Coaching Black Belt projects to successful completion

❑ Master Black Belt final examination

❑ Career-development planning and life-study plan

Master Black Belt instructor development

About 15% to 20% of an organization's Master Black Belt resources are dedicated to training. The program for developing instructional skills includes one-on-one coaching in adult-education practices and a demonstration of proficiency in classroom-presentation and project-coaching skills. Master Black Belts perform this demonstration over the course of several different waves of Black Belt and Green Belt training. These waves are conducted under supervised conditions by a seasoned Master Black Belt coach.

Master Black Belt project-manager development

About 80% to 85% of an organization's Master Black Belt resources are dedicated to three areas:

1. Coaching business leaders and process owners in the development of a portfolio of projects to be conducted.

2. Mentoring Black Belts in the accomplishment of their projects.

3. Coordination of the cross-functional collaboration required for major DMADV projects or for business-process-reengineering projects for transactional work processes.

Six Sigma network administration

Master Black Belts collaborate with the deployment champion to create a network that provides internal support and reinforcement of competence in Six Sigma skills for all participants in the Black Belt and Master Black Belt programs. Such a network should also provide advanced educational opportunities for Black Belts and Master Black Belts to ensure continuous challenges that improve the personal skills and competence of all members of the Six Sigma community.

Expectations of Master Black Belt instructors

❑ Provide instruction that is sensitive to adult learners and addresses a variety of learning modes. Each major learning objective should have an explanation, example, and exercise that are discussed among the participants. Reinforcement through homework and additional readings are positive ways for adult participants to become more fully engaged in the subject matter. If insufficient time is available during class, it is acceptable to have the exercise portion of the lesson completed as homework, provided the exercise is reviewed when the class reconvenes.

❑ Provide orientation pre-reading to give students an overview of the entire Black Belt development experience.

❑ Review each project at the beginning of the training course to determine whether it will satisfy the course's learning requirements and enable student certification.

❑ Wherever possible, illustrate all in-class examples using software tools such as Minitab or Microsoft Excel and tutor students in the applications of this software as it is used.

❑ Provide as much instruction as possible using computer aided tools. This helps anchor the application of these tools among Black Belts.

❑ Keep the four project reviews as brief as possible. Having structured requirements for each project review strengthens the benefits of sharing progress and lessons learned. The focus of the reviews should be the lessons learned from the tools, rather than the style or "graphical effects" of the presentation. (Some participants might need coaching to develop presentation skills for making clear, concise, and coherent speeches to top management.)

❑ All software should be loaded prior to the beginning of the Black Belt training. It is recommended that a software coaching session be held prior to the training so the instructor can ensure that each student has all the required software and a computer that is operational.

❑ Evening tutorials in Minitab and Microsoft Excel should be offered to provide Black Belts with an increased understanding of the way these programs work.

❑ Participants should fill out class evaluations to provide thoughtful review. Each instructor should be given the results of this feedback.

❑ Students' sponsors should be invited to attend and observe all final project presentations (realization reviews). For a student to obtain certification as a Black Belt, his/her sponsor must provide a letter certifying that the project was successful and that the performance obtained was sustained through process improvement. After completing both the training project and a second project that is conducted independently, participants receive a certificate of completion.

QUESTION  32

What should the
finance organization do?

The finance organization can play an important role at almost every decision milestone of a Six Sigma project. Two milestones—a business tollgate review and a project tollgate review—occur at the end of the Define, Analyze, and implementation steps of the DMAIC process. Only project tollgate reviews are conducted at the end of the Measure and Improve steps. The finance organization's role during each of these tollgate reviews is described below.

Define step. The objective at the end of this step is to define the project team charter and establish an initial focus for the project. Other deliverables can include a SIPOC diagram, an issue statement, a customer CTQ matrix, and a project plan. The finance organization gives guidance by providing an analysis of the magnitude of the problem and potential benefit estimates.

Measure step. The objective at the end of this step is to review the process-outcome measurement to ensure the current state of performance is represented accurately. Deliverables that the finance organization reviews include the y = f (x) analysis from business Y's to process X's, Cause & Effect/Fishbone Diagram, process baseline analysis, process benchmarking comparisons, process capability study, and measurement systems analysis (MSA). During this review, the finance organization gives guidance by providing a calculation of costs used in the analyses and determining the rough-order cost of poor quality (COPQ). Finance also validates the opportunities for potential benefits.

Analyze step. The objective at the end of this step is to review sources of controllable variation and opportunities for improving the processes that contribute most to the variation. This tollgate review results in authorization to conduct a pilot experiment to validate that proposed benefit opportunities can be realized in the routine operation of the business. Deliverables for this review include the root causes of the problem, the results expected from the proposed change, the reason for this expectation, and the benefit expected from the proposed solution. During this review, the finance organization gives guidance on the calculation of costs and provides financial validation of the proposed solution.

Improve step. The objective at the end of this step is to evaluate the results of the pilot experiment to determine the effectiveness of the proposed solution and its adequacy for answering the initial project objective. At this review, the team presents the results of the pilot study, the analysis of the proposed solution, the cost benefit observed during the pilot study, and an extrapolation of the potential benefits of full-scale implementation. During this review, the finance organization gives guidance on the financial analyses, calculates the gains observed during the pilot study, and ensures the cost-tracking system is operable for full-scale implementation.

Control step. The objective at the end of this step is to determine if the proposed changes are sustainable and to authorize the changes to the business-control system that will help to implement the recommendations. Deliverables for this review include the control plan, job-change definitions, revised process procedures and work instructions, a monitoring plan to ensure compliance with the revised process, and change-approval forms. The role of the finance organization during this review is to track the cost of making the improvements, begin monitoring the benefits to capture the value of expected project returns, and determine whether the project meets its business objectives.

Implementation. Upon implementation of all recommendations, the finance organization conducts a realization review with the project's Black Belt. The focus of this review is to validate financial and process returns. The Black Belt determines whether the recommendations are properly implemented and whether the statistical applications are being followed. The finance organization determines whether the projected benefits were captured and calculates the final benefit realized. It does this by conducting a process audit to (1) validate the performance of the changes made based on project recommendations, (2) verify that process monitoring is operating correctly, and (3) determine the project's return on investment of time and resources. The deliverable at the end of this step is a report that describes the final benefits realized, possible future gains, and local management's plan to capture these benefits (through either further projects in this area or using the process learning in other areas of the organization).

How do Green Belts contribute to Six Sigma?

Organizations can choose two different roles for their Green Belts. In both approaches, a person serves as a Green Belt part-time while working a full-time operational job.

In the first role, the Green Belt serves as a junior Black Belt, working on projects with a toolkit similar to the Black Belt's but with problems that are chosen by his/her local manager and having a smaller scope. In the second role, the Green Belt serves as an apprentice to a Black Belt. Each Green Belt is assigned a Black Belt who serves as a mentor and provides the Green Belt with on-the-job training to improve his/her proficiency and ability to operate independently. Eventually, the Green Belt can facilitate routine continuous-improvement projects.

The primary role of the Green Belt in the second approach is to facilitate the application of analysis tools that involve close participation of front-line workers. These tools include process mapping, Cause & Effect/Fishbone Diagrams, Failure Mode and Effects Analysis (FMEA), data collection, and work-process documentation. Organizations that take this route typically desire to avoid overlap between the roles of the Green Belt and Black Belt and any perceptions of their relative value to the organization based on the projects they conduct. Also, the preparation and training for the second role is much shorter than for the first role because the Black Belt provides on-the-job coaching.

Green Belts provide a "multiplier effect" for Six Sigma projects; Black Belts often complete more projects when Green Belts facilitate some of their more time-consuming analysis tasks. Also, when Green Belt training does not significantly overlap Black Belt training, employee satisfaction among these two groups is higher because they do not compete with each other for recognition and project tasks.

Typical Green Belt activities

The following list is representative of the specific tasks Green Belts typically perform while supporting a Black Belt project.

Measure

– Participate in the measurement-capability analysis.

– Collect data on measurement performance.

– Input process data into Minitab for analysis to determine baseline and Cp.

- Collect raw process information for financial analysts to calculate cost of poor quality (COPQ).
- Participate in the process-mapping team.
- Participate in the development of the FMEA.
- Assist in the preparation of the end-of-phase project report.

Analyze

- Collect data to characterize process performance for X's.
- Manage the screening tests to identify the vital few X's.
- Assist in the preparation of the end-of-phase project report.

Improve

- Conduct pilot experiments to demonstrate process improvement.
- Input data from experiments for analysis by Black Belts.
- Participate in the revised measurement-capability study.
- Assist in the preparation of the end-of-phase report.

Control

- Validate the performance of the control plan.
- Prepare instructions for use of control charts.
- Participate in the process-capability demonstration study.
- Assist in the preparation of the end-of-phase report.

Integrate

- Train front-line employees in the revised work procedures.
- Provide continuity into the implementation phase of the project.
- Assist in the revision of position descriptions and task analyses.

Standardize

- Evaluate quality-system documentation to determine the change required.
- Input the results of the project into the corporate archives for sharing.
- Assist the financial analyst in conducting data collection for the realization review.
- Assist in the documentation of work procedures.

Desirable characteristics for Green Belt candidates

The characteristics sought in a Green Belt are similar to those that are desirable for a Black Belt. They include the ability to influence colleagues without having any formal power or authority, energy and enthusiasm for problem-solving tasks, the ability to develop a systematic structure for managing work tasks, and the respect of fellow employees.

Green Belts do not need significant mathematical or statistical skills, as long as they do not have a fear of these subjects. They should have a high degree of comfort with mathematics, software, and process improvement. While experience in the use of personal computers and basic office-productivity software is essential to performing this job, tutorials can be conducted to bring candidates up to speed. Green Belts should also be capable of becoming Black Belts, should their individual desires and the needs of the organization eventually merge.

Selection of Green Belt candidates

Green Belt candidates can be nominated by the work-process owner to serve as that team's lead in working with the Black Belt. Green Belt training should also be made available to other interested employees. This ensures that those with the enthusiasm and desire to pursue this path are able to get into the pipeline without participating with their peers in a "contest" for recognition from the top management team.

Learning objectives in Green Belt training

Green Belt candidates must demonstrate the ability to do the following:

- Build Minitab databases.
- Perform basic data-manipulation tasks in Minitab.
- Transfer data to PowerPoint and Word from Minitab and Excel.
- Diagram work processes using Corel or Visio software.
- Diagram work-process failures in FMEA and fault tree analysis (FTA) models.
- Enter project-management information into Microsoft Project.
- Collect randomized data and understand sampling plans.
- Facilitate and participate in a wide variety of teams.
- Perform basic statistical analyses.
- Organize an end-of-phase project report.

Candidates must also demonstrate mastery of all the basic quality tools, competence in project-facilitation skills and team-meeting management, and an understanding of DMAIC and the actions required for delivering success.

While there is no standard process for developing Green Belts, one approach for training Black Belt apprentices uses the following five-day program:

Day One

▶ Overview of Six Sigma

▶ The role of Green Belts in the Six Sigma strategy

▶ Tasks for Green Belts in the DMAIC process

▶ Problem statements and operational definitions

▶ Meeting-management workshop

▶ Project definition and charter preparation

▶ Group facilitation

▶ Team facilitation workshop

▶ Systematic innovation process

▶ Basic graphical analysis tools

Day Two

▶ Basic statistics workshop

▶ Advanced analysis tools

▶ Six Sigma measures and calculations

▶ Minitab workshop

▶ Microsoft Excel workshop

▶ Process-management workshop

▶ Corel workshop

Day Three

▶ FMEA

▶ FTA

- Potential problem analysis
- Problem-solving process
- Methods of data collection and experimentation workshop

Day Four

- Lean-process management
- Setup-time reduction
- Work-process simplification
- Job-performance-analysis workshop
- Work-process documentation-standard writing workshop
- "Kaizen blitz" workshop

Day Five

- Microsoft Project workshop
- Preparing end-of-phase reports workshop
- End-of-course examination
- Black Belt development opportunities
- Course summary and discussion

What is the DMADV innovation process?

When an organization uses the DMAIC process, it has the ability to achieve a local maximum performance (the inherent process capability, or Cp, designed into the business process). But if this performance is not sufficient to meet the organization's competitive requirements, the organization must design the business process to be more competitive. This involves designing to a goal of flawless execution to achieve the market requirements as well as the organization's desired competitive position. An organization can design its business processes to be able to flawlessly perform at a higher level of process capability by using a design process called Design for Six Sigma (DFSS). This is represented by the process steps Define, Measure, Analyze, Design, and Verify (DMADV). The same process, with a different statistical emphasis, can be applied to the design of products and services.

DFSS Builds on DMAIC

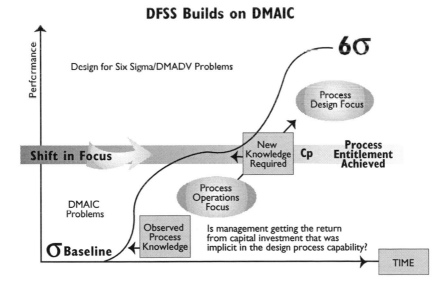

While the steps of this process have names that are similar to those of the DMAIC problem-solving process, their objectives are very different. DFSS is a methodology for designing new processes, products, or services or completely redesigning ones that already exist to achieve 3.4 defects per million opportunities or less. This comprehensive set of strategies, tactics, and tools enables an organization to characterize, quantify, and mitigate the risk involved in all phases of process, product, or service development while building quality into the design throughout this development process. DFSS is typically developed as a customized application of an organization's product-development process, integrating Six Sigma methodologies into the engineering and business requirements of product design. It is implemented as a part of an overall Six Sigma strategy and relies on an infrastructure of Black Belts to support the design projects. DFSS supplements an organization's design process.

The objective of the DMADV innovation process is to ensure that processes, products, or services consistently meet current customer needs and to anticipate the changing requirements of the future market. To meet customers' requirements (which, once known, become fixed variables), the process must be designed so that any variation still produces output that consistently meets the required performance level. When the design goal for this process capability is specified to produce failures with a probability of less than six standard deviations at this requirement, then the product can be declared to have a Six Sigma design. Once statistical data validates that the product meets this design goal, the product can be described as a Six Sigma product.

The following five-step sequence outlines the process for creating such a product. (DFSS applications for processes and services are different.)

❏ **Define.** The Define step establishes the product concept. The design-management team develops a business case for capitalizing on an opportunity in the organization's technology portfolio or product-line plan. Customer and market research helps to determine how this opportunity can address the commercial needs of the marketplace. The business case presents an initial assessment of the product concept, its commercial viability, the projected budget, and a multi-generational product plan that identifies how new product variants will be sequenced for introduction into the market. After the initial conceptual design is reviewed, the product budget and project plan are approved. A development team is then assigned to staff the project. (For more details on the Define step, see Question 35.)

❏ **Measure.** The Measure step evaluates the market requirements and potential market demand for the product. During this step, research is planned to determine customer needs and competitive performance and to identify features and options that make the product unique. The team also seeks to identify design elements that satisfy customer requirements. This step in the design process is documented using quality function deployment (QFD) matrices and design scorecards, which record the progress of the project. Design control is managed through tollgate reviews of critical activities to ensure that adequate progress is made toward the planned product-launch date. (For more details on the Measure step, see Question 36.)

❏ **Analyze.** The Analyze step completes product characterization. It includes several key activities: functional analysis of the product's features and their capability to address identified customer requirements, benchmarking of these features' performance, conceptual design of the product, process maps of the production and service-delivery processes, and a design-requirement specification. The tollgate review at the end of this step evaluates the design scorecard and compares the design requirements with the business plan to authorize the detailed product design. (For more details on the Analyze step, see Question 37.)

❑ **Design.** In the Design step, detailed process maps are created for the production facility's layout and the engineering detail of the product specification. All the critical process parameters are identified, failure analysis is conducted to determine potential risks, capability analysis is conducted to determine design robustness, and statistical analysis is used to establish tolerances for critical parameters. Value analysis is conducted to ensure that the product value proposition is optimized. Reliability testing of prototypes is also conducted to demonstrate growth in the stability of the design and its readiness for the marketplace. (For more details on the Design step, see Question 38.)

❑ **Verify.** The Verify step engages the customer in product testing through pilot tests that demonstrate the marketability of the product and its production readiness. Pilot tests also verify the details for transition to full production and the implementation of the control procedures for routine production after ramp-up to the full forecast volume is achieved. The control plan for the product is embedded in its assembly procedures, test procedures, and acceptance criteria. Upon completion of this step, product development transitions to full production, which is marked by an official product launch. (For more details on the Verify step, see Question 39.)

How does the Define step of DMADV work?

Objectives

The three objectives of the Define step are to:

1. Specify a business case and a design concept for development of a new product.

2. Define how the product structure and subsequent releases of variant designs will change due to the organization's product-development plan.

3. Establish a target competitive position for the new product in the organization's product portfolio.

Definition

The Define step evaluates market feasibility and risk associated with alternative concepts for new product development and establishes the scope and the charter for selected projects.

Inputs to the Define step

The figure on the next page illustrates the inputs to the Define step. Inputs on the left side of the figure come from the prior Recognize step; those on the top describe concepts, principles, or methods used to facilitate the Define step; and those on the bottom identify the tools that are used. The outputs on the right lead to step two in the DMADV process, the Measure step. The horizontal input/output flow in the figure indicates the linkage among the five DMADV steps.

Thought Map for the Define Step

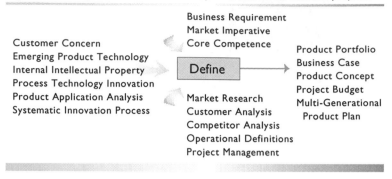

Define: Evaluates the market feasibility and risk of alternative concepts for product development and establishes scope and charter for selected projects.

Customer Concern
Emerging Product Technology
Internal Intellectual Property
Process Technology Innovation
Product Application Analysis
Systematic Innovation Process

Business Requirement
Market Imperative
Core Competence

Define

Market Research
Customer Analysis
Competitor Analysis
Operational Definitions
Project Management

Product Portfolio
Business Case
Product Concept
Project Budget
Multi-Generational
Product Plan

Questions to ask during the Define step

▶ What customer experiences with our products and services need to be improved from the customers' perspective?

▶ Where is the market going? What developments are happening that can threaten our current position?

▶ What competitive moves are taking place that can shift the market-share balance?

▶ What business priorities of our customers can our products and services fill better than those of our competitors? Where is our advantage, and how can we extend it?

▶ What unspoken needs of our customers have not yet been recognized and will yield a competitive advantage if we are the first in the market to fulfill them?

▶ How can our portfolio of intellectual property and licensable emerging technology be applied in an innovative way to our products and services?

▶ Are there technology areas that we require in the future to which we currently have no access?

▶ What innovation is possible that could make our customers' lives easier, smarter, quicker, and less defect-prone?

▶ Can our core competence be leveraged into a greater advantage over our competitors?

Define step deliverables

▶ Technology acquisition plan

▶ Product portfolio

▶ Product business case (including design concept and product budget)

▶ Multi-generational product plan

Analysis tools

The following techniques support the investigations done during the Define step.

▶ Six Sigma DMAIC toolkit

▶ Customer surveys

▶ Market research

▶ Focus groups

▶ Technology assessment

▶ SWOT analysis

▶ Projection of the diffusion of innovation

▶ Market level forecasting

▶ Product-level forecasting

▶ Break-even time payback analysis

▶ Risk-based decision making

▶ Road mapping

▶ Multi-generational product plan

Define step activity checklist

▶ Study market trends and customer preferences.

▶ Evaluate competitive moves and capabilities.

▶ Assess technology capabilities and development opportunities.

▶ Engage the innovative power of the organization by conducting a creative dialogue about the external business environment.

▶ Do a SWOT analysis of the current situation to find unique opportunities that leverage the organization's core competence and portfolio of technologies.

▶ Evaluate opportunities and forecast potential market demands.

▶ Translate decisions into a product-development road map embedded into a multi-generational product plan based on the R&D investment-payback potential.

A Systematic Innovation Process

Seize an Opportunity

Build a Cohort

Select a Tool

Define Roles

Systematic
Innovation Process   (SIP)

Design the Event

Obtain Resources

Creative Dialogue

Opening Session	Sorting Session	Closing Session

Define step summary

The objective of the Define step of DMADV is to study an organization's competitors, markets, and technology to discover general trends of interest and determine an opportunity for new product development that can create an enduring competitive advantage. Business leaders commission research into markets, customers, and competitors to develop background information for constructing a business case. An organization's innovative power is engaged through creative dialogue to define a road map for new product development. This is then presented as a multi-generational product plan.

How does the Measure step of DMADV work?

Objective

Translate a design concept into a product concept that is aligned with the needs of customers in the product's targeted market segments.

Definition

The Measure step identifies expectations of targeted customers through in-depth customer analysis, determines which product functions are aligned to these expectations, and makes the product as competitive as possible via alternative designs.

Inputs to the Measure step

The figure below illustrates the inputs to the Measure step. Inputs on the left side of the figure come from the prior Define step; those on the top describe concepts, principles, or methods used to facilitate the Measure step; and those on the bottom identify the tools that are used. The outputs on the right lead to step three in the DMADV process, the Analyze step. The horizontal input/output flow in the figure indicates the linkage among the five DMADV steps.

Thought Map for the Measure Step

Questions to ask during the Measure step

▶ What specific product or service features are required by specific customer segments?

▶ How do requirements, needs, and expectations differ among various types of customers (i.e., market segment, application persona, decision level, etc.)?

▶ Which features have the highest priority as customer requirements?

▶ Which features provide a competitive advantage according to a Kano analysis?

▶ How do the top-priority customer needs translate into critical-to-quality (CTQ) product features?

▶ Where are there opportunities to develop performance advantages over competing products' features?

▶ How are high-level functions related to customers' CTQ priorities?

▶ What types of risk are anticipated in product development? Where are these risks most intensive?

▶ Which customer segments make up the target audience for the product or service? How do these segments relate to the historical market acceptance for these types of products?

Measure step deliverables

▶ Conceptual definition of the product

▶ Design scorecard for the Measure step

▶ R&D project-management plan

▶ QFD A-level matrix

Analysis tools

The following techniques support the investigations performed during the Measure step.

▶ DMAIC toolkit

▶ QFD

▶ Kano analysis

▶ Customer relationship management

▶ Customer segmentation analysis

▶ Consumer persona creation

▶ Customer-needs analysis/voice of the customer (VOC) analysis

▶ Operational definition

▶ Competitive product analysis

- Performance scorecard for the Define step
- Multi-generational product plan

Measure step activity checklist

- Perform detailed CTQ analysis based on preliminary customer/market research.
- Conduct Kano analysis of customer requirements.
- Conduct competitive product analysis.
- Translate priority customer requirements into operational definitions.
- Record all observations in an A-level QFD matrix.
- Evaluate product-development risks based on the products' conceptual design.
- Complete the performance scorecard for the Define step.

Measure step summary

The objective of the Measure step of DMADV is to conduct very detailed analyses of customer requirements and then translate the most promising requirements into design requirements, which are recorded in a QFD matrix as a product concept.

How does the Analyze step of DMADV work?

Objectives

Translate a product concept into a high-level product design and characterize the technological and business risks associated with full-scale product development.

Definition

The Analyze step completes the high-level design of the product, demonstrates market suitability of the design concept, determines the degree of technological risk associated with further development, and develops initial plans for marketing the product.

Inputs to the Analyze step

The figure below illustrates the inputs to the Analyze step. Inputs on the left side of the figure come from the prior Measure step; those on the top describe concepts, principles, or methods used to facilitate the Analyze step; and those on the bottom identify the tools that are used. The outputs on the right lead to step four in the DMADV process, the Design step. The horizontal input/output flow in the figure indicates the linkage among the five DMADV steps.

Thought Map for the Analyze Step

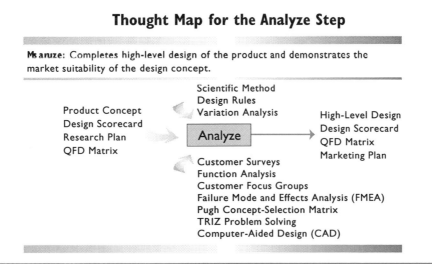

Analyze: Completes high-level design of the product and demonstrates the market suitability of the design concept.

Product Concept
Design Scorecard
Research Plan
QFD Matrix

Scientific Method
Design Rules
Variation Analysis

Analyze

High-Level Design
Design Scorecard
QFD Matrix
Marketing Plan

Customer Surveys
Function Analysis
Customer Focus Groups
Failure Mode and Effects Analysis (FMEA)
Pugh Concept-Selection Matrix
TRIZ Problem Solving
Computer-Aided Design (CAD)

Questions to ask during the Analyze step

▶ What product features are necessary to support the design requirements?

▶ How do these features translate into an acceptable product for targeted customers?

▶ What can go wrong at the system level with the operation of these product features?

▶ What are innovative ways to implement these features into a high-level design?

▶ How should we choose the best design from among alternatives?

▶ How can we reduce the product's time to market through the use of computer-aided design (CAD) tools?

Analyze step deliverables

▶ High-level product design

▶ Design scorecard for the Analyze step

▶ Market-development plan and project-management plan

▶ QFD B-level matrix

Analysis tools

The following techniques support the investigations performed during the Analyze step.

▶ DMAIC toolkit

▶ Function Analysis System Technique (FAST)

▶ TRIZ approach to inventive problem solving

▶ System-level Failure Mode and Effects Analysis (FMEA)

▶ Fault tree analysis (FTA)

▶ Pugh matrix

▶ Customer surveys

▶ Customer focus groups

▶ Quality function deployment (QFD)

▶ CAD

Analyze step activity checklist

▶ Allocate the critical-to-quality (CTQ) requirements to product functions.

▶ Define the functional details necessary to deliver the features customers require.

▶ Consider innovative ways to implement the functional design.

- Evaluate failure opportunities in the functional design and find countermeasures to eliminate opportunities for defects.

- Evaluate alternative design concepts based on the management criteria for success in delivering the product to the marketplace.

- Conduct customer research to determine the relative value of alternative designs.

- Translate the product-design requirements into functional requirements for parts design.

- Begin the QFD B-level matrix.

- Initiate the CAD design of the product with the high-level system architecture.

Analyze step summary

The objective of the Analyze step of DMADV is to translate a rough product concept into a high-level product design that is ready for detailed engineering-level design as well as market planning.

How does the Design step of DMADV work?

Objective

Translate a high-level product design into a detailed engineering-level design that is ready for hard tooling and preparation for full-scale production.

Definition

The Design step develops detailed product design and control plans that ensure robust performance in the eventual production environment. It also prepares the project for management's final design decision to implement the product in full-scale operation.

Inputs to the Design step

The figure below illustrates the inputs to the Design step. Inputs on the left side of the figure come from the prior Analyze step; those on the top describe concepts, principles, or methods used to facilitate the Design step; and those on the bottom identify the tools that are used. The outputs on the right lead to step five in the DMADV process, the Verify step. The horizontal input/output flow in the figure indicates the linkage among the five DMADV steps.

Thought Map for the Design Step

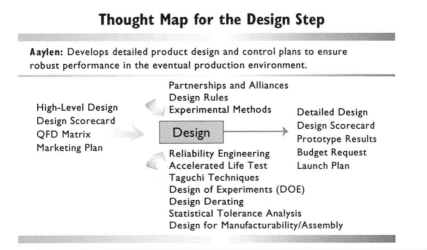

Aaylen: Develops detailed product design and control plans to ensure robust performance in the eventual production environment.

High-Level Design
Design Scorecard
QFD Matrix
Marketing Plan

Partnerships and Alliances
Design Rules
Experimental Methods

Design

Reliability Engineering
Accelerated Life Test
Taguchi Techniques
Design of Experiments (DOE)
Design Derating
Statistical Tolerance Analysis
Design for Manufacturability/Assembly

Detailed Design
Design Scorecard
Prototype Results
Budget Request
Launch Plan

Questions to ask during the Design step

▶ How should the product parts be designed to deliver the required functionality?

▶ How can the parts be designed for high reliability?

▶ What is the expected market life of this product?

▶ What is the best operating envelope for the critical design parameters?

▶ What tolerance limits will produce the most reliable product design?

▶ How can the parts fit together in a way that reduces production-cycle time?

▶ Is the product ready to be considered for full-scale production?

▶ What is the plan for launching the product in the marketplace?

▶ What is the plan for tooling the product for full-scale production?

▶ Are the production facilities ready to accept the product?

▶ Have the production procedures been written so that all jobs are specified?

Design step deliverables

▶ Detailed engineering design

▶ Design scorecard for the Design step

▶ Prototype results from product beta-testing with customers

▶ New-product-launch plan from marketing

▶ Budget request for full-scale implementation and product launch

▶ QFD C-level matrix

Analysis tools

The following techniques support the investigations performed during the Design step.

▶ DMAIC toolkit

▶ Product-level FMEA

▶ Reliability engineering

▶ Accelerated life testing

▶ Taguchi analysis

▶ Design of experiments (DOE)

▶ Statistical tolerance analysis

▶ Design for manufacturing/assembly (DFMA)

▶ Computer-aided design/computer-aided manufacturing (CAD/CAM)

Design step activity checklist

▶ Allocate failure opportunities to product parts and develop a budget for testing.

▶ Conduct prototype testing to demonstrate the range of functionality and expected life of the product under normal operating conditions.

▶ Define operating envelopes and tolerance bands of specification parameters.

▶ Analyze product parts and modules to ensure proper manufacture and assembly.

▶ Translate all design documents into appropriate CAD/CAM programs.

▶ Conduct a full-scale design review of the product's production readiness.

Design step summary

The objective of the Design step of DMADV is to translate a high-level design into an engineered product that has been tested as a prototype and found to be ready for full-scale production.

How does the Verify step of DMADV work?

Objective

Translate a detailed engineering-level design into a product that is offered to customers.

Definition

The Verify step validates product-design plans and provides formal documentation for full-scale production in preparation for giving the design to a process owner.

Inputs to the Verify step

The figure below illustrates the inputs to the Verify step. Inputs on the left side of the figure come from the prior Design step; those on the top describe concepts, principles, or methods used to facilitate the Verify step; and those on the bottom identify the tools that are used. The outputs on the right lead to the implementation phase. The horizontal input/output flow in the figure indicates the linkage among the five DMADV steps.

Thought Map for the Verify Step

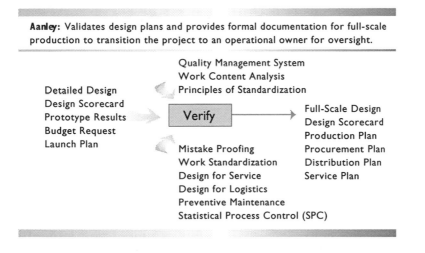

Aanley: Validates design plans and provides formal documentation for full-scale production to transition the project to an operational owner for oversight.

Quality Management System
Work Content Analysis
Principles of Standardization

Detailed Design
Design Scorecard
Prototype Results
Budget Request
Launch Plan

Verify

Full-Scale Design
Design Scorecard
Production Plan
Procurement Plan
Distribution Plan
Service Plan

Mistake Proofing
Work Standardization
Design for Service
Design for Logistics
Preventive Maintenance
Statistical Process Control (SPC)

Questions to ask during the Verify step

▶ What are the opportunities for defects in the production process?

▶ What countermeasures are possible to mistake-proof the production process?

▶ What detailed procedures must be followed to produce the product?

▶ What is the strategy for servicing the product?

▶ What is the plan for distributing the product and ensuring market availability?

▶ How capable is the production process? What is its full-scale entitlement?

▶ Is the measurement system sensitive enough to detect significant changes in the critical process-control parameters?

▶ Are the maintenance requirements for production equipment established? Has a cycle time been prepared to anticipate problems and prevent failures?

▶ Has automated test equipment been implemented to decrease the non-value-added time required for in-process testing?

▶ Is statistical process control implemented in conjunction with engineering process control to ensure that the production process consistently delivers the quality level it was designed to produce?

▶ Is there a plan to review all early product returns to ensure that problems are fixed as soon as they are detected?

▶ Are there any "showstoppers" that would delay the product's release to the market?

Verify step deliverables

▶ Full-scale product design

▶ Design scorecard for the Verify step

▶ Production plan

▶ Procurement plan

▶ Distribution plan

▶ Service plan

▶ QFD D-level matrix

Analysis tools

The following techniques support the investigations performed during the Verify step.

▶ DMAIC toolkit

▶ Process-level FMEA

▶ Poka-yoke mistake-proofing

▶ Work standardization

- Design for service
- Design for logistics
- Preventive maintenance
- Measurement systems analysis (MSA)
- Statistical process control (SPC)
- Process capability analysis
- Computer-automated test equipment

Verify step activity checklist

- Prepare a failure analysis of the production process.
- Mistake-proof the process.
- Define production assembly work standards and train operators.
- Develop logistic plans for product service and distribution.
- Develop a preventive maintenance program for the production equipment.
- Evaluate measurement capability at work-process control points and implement a closed-loop control system for automated test and engineering process control.
- Track the ramp-up of production from initial process capability to the design level of process capability (Cp).
- Develop a launch quality plan to capture early product failures for analysis and rapid corrective action.

Verify step summary

The objective of the Verify step of DMADV is to translate an engineered product into full-scale production detail and transition the Design for Six Sigma (DFSS) project to the daily management system for routine commercial operation.

How does Six Sigma
align with daily work?

The objective of any organization's management system is to deliver desired results. When this is done in a consistent, predictable manner, the organization is considered to be operating in a state of control. In such a situation, all employees know what to do, how to do it, how to evaluate their work output, and how to correct their work processes to maintain performance and prevent errors or defects from occurring. In addition, their work is designed to flow seamlessly from one activity to another, without excess loss of time or money, while maintaining the required quality of their combined output.

Such a state of control does not normally happen without the heroic efforts of the entire business. This includes involvement of employees at all levels (from executives to front-line workers), integration of work-process design (from suppliers, to work processes, to the customers), and alignment of the measurement system (from the business Y's to the process X's).

Creating a daily management system

A daily management system must define how a company's process organization works, as well as how its functional organizations deliver support services to the business processes. To create such a system, a process architecture flow must be established to map the end-to-end customer-delivery process and link all the functional processes to the business processes. Such a map includes different points where progress is measured and where control can be exercised. It also defines specific work processes whose activities should be documented in a standard operating practice or work procedure. This type of process map is called an *enterprise model*. Some of the specific tools used to create a daily management system include the following:

 ▶ Customer expectations and market requirements

 ▶ Balanced scorecard and customer dashboard measurement systems

 ▶ Regulatory compliance legislation

 ▶ Business productivity improvement goals

 ▶ Financial management targets

 ▶ ISO 9000 work-process documentation

- Lean-enterprise 5S workplace streamlining and housekeeping
- Mistake-proofing of work procedures
- Statistical process control (SPC)
- Engineering process control
- Objectives cascade and project deployment
- Responsibility and accountability delegation
- Delegation of decision rights and empowerment limits
- Competence and training-process assessment
- Personnel performance-evaluation systems
- Complaint-response systems
- Corrective-action process

Effective implementation and execution of a comprehensive daily management system result in consistent, predictable performance.

Relationship of daily management to Six Sigma

Daily management systems fulfill an organization's basic objectives: increasing the value of shareholder investment and satisfying customers. While striving to achieve these goals, an organization must also keep its attention focused on delivering expected short-term performance and strengthening its long-term capability.

To maintain this balance between short-term and long-term performance, it is essential that the daily management system be strengthened by periodic strategic efforts that deliver long-term strength. This is the objective of the Japanese strategic change project–selection process called *hoshin kanri*, which supplements the daily management system called *nichijo kanri*. While all of an organization's work is specified in the daily management system, strategic changes to this system are made as projects that are accomplished by special team efforts using resources managed under the hoshin construct.

Hoshin planning is the strategic management of business change. It is equivalent to the Six Sigma Recognize step, which precedes the DMAIC project definition and execution process (see Question 8). The Improve, Control, and implementation steps of the DMAIC process all support the daily management system. Taken as a whole, the Six Sigma project-management approach is similar to the Japanese process, delivering daily performance and long-term strength.

Controls can be used to ensure an organization's constancy of purpose and repeatability of performance in mission-critical areas. Achieving this degree of control requires that two aspects of the management process—business control and statistical control—are effectively designed and implemented. These two controls must be integrated to ensure sustained achievement of business objectives.

The next section examines each type of control independently and explains how they fit together in a practical and efficient daily management system.

Daily management and business control

Effective business control is essential to any daily management process. Five requirements for effective business control are listed below.

1. Managers must lead by example. No management system can endure leaders who do not apply the same principles to themselves that they apply to their workers.

2. An organization must manage by process. Organizations that do not use process management become introspective and self-seeking, and consequently they lose their competitive edge.

3. Workers must monitor measurements. Measuring in itself is not enough; it is essential to use measures that enable an organization to learn more about the business and choose its direction more carefully.

4. Managers must evaluate progress. Performance management without effective decision making results in frustration for the entire organization. Using measurement systems to identify and effect change in routine operations makes workers actually believe such methods can make a difference.

5. Managers must adapt to their environment. Excellence is not merely the product of a good process map, measurement system, or self-assessment scheme; it comes when leaders lead by example and hold other employees accountable for following that example.

Below are details about how these five factors are involved in designing a daily management system for business control.

1. Leading by example. Leading by example means that a manager is a role model for the type of behavior that is desirable throughout the entire organization. The actions of the top management team must be consistent with the organization's strategies, beliefs, and values. Leaders must establish trust in the organization, act with integrity, and put service to the organization beyond their own self-interest.

Failure to establish trust results in an objection that many organizations have to strategic change: lack of management commitment. Executive commitment requires that leaders do the following:

❑ Allocate time for activities that are within their range of responsibility.

❑ Display a positive attitude toward improving the organization.

❑ Be visible and involved in planning and evaluating work performance.

❑ Assess the readiness of the organization and its employees to accept their own responsibility for daily management activities.

❑ Verify that employees apply the necessary control steps in their daily work and that they react appropriately to out-of-control conditions.

❑ Lead the business unit in conducting self-assessments of current state performance.

❑ Express meaningful appreciation in a fair manner to all employees who make desired behavioral or organizational-performance changes. This means not just rewards, but also personal acts of recognition.

2. Managing by process. Making the transition from a functional focus in management to managing by process is the most critical change for an organization to undertake. It is fundamental when making customers the most crucial determinant of an organization's sustained business success.

Processes are collections of activities that define how work is done and the set of tasks that together deliver value to customers. In organizations with a functional focus, the emphasis is placed on keeping the boss happy by giving other people work to accomplish. This internal focus feeds a hierarchical organization that emphasizes layers of reporting rather than a focus on the customer. In contrast, organizations managed by process seek to achieve functional excellence and work with their peer organizations as a team to focus on meeting customers' needs.

An organization managed by process succeeds through *customer intimacy:* knowing what customers want and providing it in a flawless manner. To achieve this level of performance, an organization must master the basic skills of process management, which are listed below.

❑ Make process steps visible and understand clearly what is required of each segment in the customer-delivery chain.

❑ Measure performance of the process at each critical junction point capable of characterizing performance regarding input, process steps, or output or results measures.

❑ Optimize flow across the process by eliminating bottlenecks and decreasing setup and waiting times across all activities.

❑ Evaluate progress to ensure that a common direction is maintained and that the rate of progress is satisfactory in all areas.

Managing by process begins by charting work processes to design the map by which work flows across functions in response to customer or market demands. Charting processes identifies all the key inputs, outputs, process steps, and performance measures.

Such work-flow analysis can be conducted at different levels of abstraction. For the highest level, which requires a simple working model that explains how a business operates, a block diagram is a suitable tool. When a description of how work flows across functions is needed, a deployment diagram is useful. When mapping measures to process flows, a thought-process map is appropriate. Each of these tools helps to characterize processes and determine how to sequence the activities and establish the relationship among the process variables that results in optimal performance. Analysis is needed to define the necessary set of process measures and establish appropriate performance levels.

Once performance levels have been established for the critical process parameters, the objective is to define the conditions that will keep performance at the optimal level. These conditions are the fundamental aspects of the business-control system used for daily management. Work-flow charting helps with the design and documentation of work processes and builds business literacy. A work-flow chart is a blueprint for the entire business process. It is constructed from the customers' perspective, since customers' requirements describe the goals of the process.

After the management team designs a business model to document the work flow, the team uses a measurement system to generate action that keeps the organization aligned toward its business objectives. Management measures and improves the key areas of routine business control by doing the following:

❑ Monitoring periodic progress toward achieving results against a set of expectations, benchmarks, and performance indicators that define a desired operating envelope.

❑ Evaluating progress to ensure that resources are managed properly and that the desired results are consistently obtained.

Each of these responsibilities requires the creation of a robust measurement system for work-process monitoring.

3. Monitoring measurements. To monitor work-flow measurements efficiently, an organization needs a measurement system that is aligned with its performance objectives. Tracking specific performance indicators gives the most immediate feedback on the effectiveness of the daily management system and on how well business goals are being met. These fundamental day-to-day and month-to-month indicators help an organization to spot problems before they become major business issues and help to pinpoint improvement opportunities that will enable the organization to better meet customer needs.

There are two types of performance indicators. The first, results indicators (Y variables), evaluate process output and describe how well a process is meeting customer expectations or business goals. Often external benchmarks are used for comparison to ensure that these goals remain competitive and that expectations are refreshed relative to changes in market conditions and competitors' moves.

The second type of performance indicator is process measures. They evaluate either the input to a process or the in-process performance. These measures provide the earliest warning of potential customer problems. Input measures describe how well suppliers meet a company's expectations as a customer and indicate how well the daily management system is working at the interface with the company's suppliers. In-process measures indicate potential defects in the system, places where the process is inefficient because excess time or resources are consumed, or the existence of significant opportunities for performance improvement (i.e., defect, cost, or cycle-time reduction).

Tracking these measures provides insight into the degree to which customer expectations are being met and the progress that processes are making toward achieving their performance objectives. A monitoring system must be consistent in measurement and action and have a simple measurement structure so that the required action is clear at all levels.

Even when a measurement system operates effectively, it is essential for management to monitor its performance and conduct regular self-assessments. This ensures that the results reflect real-world conditions and that there are no changes in the underlying process or business assumptions that would require a departure from the current strategic direction.

4. Evaluating progress. Evaluating progress is essential for making progress. Evaluating improvement progress has two dimensions: a measurement system for evaluating results, and self-assessments regarding consistency in executing daily work processes. Progress evaluation includes stewardship, an accountability process whereby measurement of compliance is reported and improvement actions are identified. Stewardship focuses on the management of financial, physical, and process resources to achieve targeted performance requirements.

Progress evaluation also includes operational reviews, which scrutinize performance measures to ensure that work is being carried out and that it meets the plan. Discoveries of any shortfalls or over-achievement require an explanation and potential actions. Progress evaluation also includes current-state analysis, which ensures that all work processes are in compliance with business requirements and regulatory constraints.

5. Adapting to the environment. Managers need to establish an environment that reinforces and sustains the daily management system so that performance objectives are achieved and compliance with all business and regulatory requirements is ensured. Performance assessments are best conducted as a normal part of daily work activities.

Daily management and statistical control

Statistical thinking seeks to minimize variation in the way work is performed. It is possible to manage work processes so that their outcomes have minimal variation and are highly predictable. Statistical control is achieved when (1) a process consistently operates close to its targeted customer-performance requirement over a sustained period of time and (2) any observed process variation is within the customers' tolerance range regarding performance quality.

Six Sigma projects identify a business concern causing a significant problem and transform it into a statistical problem. This problem is resolved by identifying the factors that shift the average performance or increase process variation. By breaking down the work-process measurement system from the business Y's to the process X's (which are measured in quality, cost, and time parameters), the relationship of the measurement system to the statistical problem can be established.

The analytical objective of a Six Sigma project is the identification of the process X's that should be the focal point of the work-process improvement project. This is done by using "drill-down" logic to discover the greatest sources of variation and then determining how to control them to minimize the variation. By doing this, the Black Belt bridges the gap between statistical control and business control in a way that achieves practical control. Practical control comes from eliminating the root cause of a problem and integrating business and statistical controls. This is the formula for sustainable success.

Daily management and sustained performance

The ultimate success of a business is measured financially by return on net assets, earnings per share, return on investment, return on capital employed, operating profit, and cash flow. Success is measured commercially by the organization's sustainable reputation in its principal market (through brand value, which is the market's sustained confidence that the business can provide enduring customer satisfaction).

To achieve sustainable performance, an organization must succeed in both of these dimensions and use planned actions to deliver this outcome. Sustained success results from sound management in an organization's daily work processes. An organization can aspire to sustainable progress toward its vision only when conscious management action delivers the desired performance. Sustainable performance does not result from serendipitous activity that delivers results without any relationship to the organization's plans or actions. When management does not take specific actions in its daily management system to generate the performance that it achieves, there is a risk that the organization will not be able to sustain its success in the future. That type of success comes from luck, not from execution excellence.

How does Six Sigma relate to ISO 9000?

ISO 9000 was originally developed to help standardize quality audits of industry suppliers. Prior to a broad industry acceptance of ISO 9000 as a minimum acceptable standard, suppliers had to meet or exceed a wide variety of incompatible quality standards, some of which defined similar methods in different ways. To make life easier for suppliers, ISO 9000, a standard quality-management system, was developed.

Like Six Sigma, ISO 9000 is a way to control processes to ensure repeatable performance across working shifts and between organizations that share similar tasks or collaborate on joint tasks for customers. Today's version of this standard, ISO 9000:2000, requires organizations to focus on their customers, to continuously improve while using a documented quality-management system to sustain gains made during improvement efforts, and to ensure consistent application of similar work processes in different business areas. This mirrors the business-control application that Six Sigma requires during the DMAIC Control step and during the DMADV implementation phase.

An organization doesn't need to have an ISO 9000 quality management system in place before it begins a Six Sigma initiative. However, undertaking a Six Sigma initiative can definitely help an organization make progress toward achieving an ISO 9000 certification.

How should a reward/recognition system work?

Reward and recognition during a Six Sigma initiative encourage role-model behavior that leads to successful implementation. For an initiative to be sustained over a long period of time, it is essential that employees feel good about the strategic value of their work (see Question 5) and that the work of Black Belts and project teams be recognized for its valuable contribution to improving organizational performance.

Human-resource specialists and staff-compensation managers must develop an appropriate reward/recognition system that is aligned with their organization's culture and compensation policies. Companies implementing Six Sigma programs must devise reward/recognition systems that are fair and equitable to all employees involved in a project. These systems allow project results to be shared across an organization and provide incentive from peer recognition of high-quality work.

Principles of a reward/recognition system

The following individuals should be recognized in reward/recognition efforts:

❑ Managers who sponsor projects.

❑ Black Belts who conduct project analyses.

❑ Team members who work with Black Belts on analyses or with process owners on implementation.

❑ Master Black Belts who serve as technical reviewers of projects.

The efforts of the organization as a whole should be reinforced. Thus, it is important for business leaders to find meaningful ways to express appreciation in a fair manner to all employees who make desired behavioral or organizational-performance changes. This means not just financial rewards, but recognition of events and personal acts that reinforce desired behavior and facilitate a sustained Six Sigma effort.

Below is a list of some basic principles for a reward/recognition system.

1. There must be rewards for results. If rewards are given to shareholders only (in the form of shareholder value) and employees receive nothing from their extra efforts, then Six Sigma team members will not feel committed to making a continuing improvement effort. When employees are given an ownership stake in the organization, they find it easier to accept the shareholders' perspective.

2. Cooperation must be the basis for working together. Therefore, reward and recognition must be done fairly throughout the organization, or else it will undermine the collaborative work environment.

3. Employees must feel secure in their employment. Those who support the program must be rewarded through continuing employment opportunities. Their job might change, but they must not feel that their livelihood is threatened. A reward/recognition system should include an explicit statement about management policies pertaining to any downsizing that occurs due to productivity gains from Six Sigma projects. Such policies should be part of the foundation of a reward/recognition system.

4. Business leaders must work to establish a climate of fairness regarding opportunities for reward and recognition. Refer to Question 5 for a list of basic principles of fairness.

Recognition is more meaningful to employees when it is given with an appropriate public ceremony during which respected business leaders present rewards. Recognition must be timely and frequent to ensure that the desired behaviors being acknowledged are reinforced by the presentation.

One criticism of reward programs is that they do not extend effectively into public-service, government, or nonprofit organizations. One remedy is to tie rewards to the cost savings derived from project work rather than tying them to the creation of profits. When these organizations do this, many of the problems they encounter with reward programs are resolved.

A Sample Six Sigma reward/recognition program

Dow Chemical created the Six Sigma reward program outlined below. It is a suitable prototype for other organizations' reward systems.

❑ Black Belts receive deferred stock awards in recognition of performance on project work. Awards are based on a formula using financial return captured by the realization review.

❑ Master Black Belts receive stock options as an incentive for continued employment. This ensures long-term strength of the Six Sigma program.

❑ Teams are awarded special bonuses for their participation in successful projects. Bonuses are based on a financial formula with a scale that increases with total realized return.

❑ All employees receive variable incentive pay (e.g., profit sharing) based on the overall financial improvement of the organization.

❑ Business leaders and executive sponsors receive rewards as the Six Sigma performance criteria are included in the organization's variable compensation and bonus programs.

▶ TIP

Below is a list of opportunities for recognition in a Six Sigma program and suitable awards.

- Selection as a candidate for Black Belt training: nomination letter from CEO or top divisional executive.
- Completion of first project: pin and training certificate signed by instructor and deployment champion.
- Participation in a Six Sigma project: T-shirt or coffee mug presented to all team members upon completion of project (i.e., it is released to the process owner for implementation).
- Completion of Black Belt qualification requirements: certificate signed by CEO and supervising Master Black Belt instructor, presented at an award-ceremony dinner.
- Completion of fifth, tenth, fifteenth, twentieth, or twenty-fifth project: plaque presented to all project participants.
- Realization of savings for milestones of one, two, three, four, or five million dollars: replica stock certificate signed by CEO and board chairman and presented to all project participants.
- Winner of Six Sigma Project of the Month competition: photo of senior and local executive recognizing the project champion, Black Belt, and team members, given to all participants and published in the organization's newsletter.
- Winner of Six Sigma Project of the Year competition: trophy given to Black Belt and all team members, with a news story and a photo of the team released to the local press.
- Winner of divisional competition for Six Sigma deployment excellence: trophy given to the group in the organization that maximizes the criteria for deployment of Six Sigma.

Career planning as a form of recognition

An important way of recognizing Black Belts is to effectively reintegrate them into the organization after their tour of duty in a Six Sigma initiative. American Express, for example, created an "engagement strategy" for reintegrating Black Belts into the company after their work was done. The purpose of such a strategy is to provide sound career counseling for successful Black Belts, who are high-potential employees. In addition to creating a good feeling among Black Belts after their tour of duty, providing this counseling does the following:

❑ It provides a redeployment strategy for individuals who wish to return to the business after completing their full-time assignment as a Black Belt. It ensures that their assignment within the business will be fair, equitable, career enhancing, and in compliance with all corporate personnel policies.

❑ It assures Black Belts that career enrichment and retention opportunities exist for individuals who choose to remain in the Black Belt role after their initial assignment period.

QUESTION

What Six Sigma metrics should be used?

To align a measurement system to the stakeholder criteria for business success using the y = f (x) approach (see Question 12), shareholder value and brand value must be linked to front-line measures of process performance. To achieve sustained performance or significantly increase performance growth, an organization must make sure that quality, cost, and time are components of its work-process measurement system. The measures for an "atomic level of work" are shown in the figure below.

Work-Process Scorecard

Measurement Component Value	Baseline	Benchmark	Current	Target
Theoretical Cycle Time (TCT)				
Actual Cycle Time (ACT)				
Value-Added Time (VAT)				
Non-Value-Added Time (1) (NVAT1)				
Non-Value-Added Time (2) (NVAT2)				
Process Productivity (RTY)				
Defects				
A				
B				
C				
D				
E				
Process Capability (Cp and Cpk)				
Process Sigma (long- and short-term)				
Cost of Poor Quality (COPQ)				

The measures in the above figure, which are described below, are recorded at four levels: (1) the initial performance baseline, (2) the external benchmark level of performance, (3) the current level of performance, and (4) the targeted improvement based on the process-design capability.

❑ **Theoretical cycle time (TCT).** The sum of the value-added cycle time plus the required non-value-added cycle time. The ratio of TCT to actual cycle time indicates the amount of improvement needed for the process to become lean.

- **Actual cycle time (ACT).** The observed total cycle time of a work process, spanning from the time a unit begins the process to the time it successfully completes the process. ACT is the sum of the value-added cycle time plus both categories of non-value-added cycle time plus the time spent by a product or process waiting in a queue for activity to occur.

- **Value-added time (VAT).** The process-performance time that adds value from the customers' perspective. VAT also refers to the time during which work is done right the first time, requiring no further processing or action to become complete or ready for transfer to the next process step. A value-adding process step contributes to the improved fit, function, or form of the product or service that it produces.

- **Non-value-added time (1) (NVAT1).** This term refers to non-value-adding activities that consume time, drain resources, and occupy space in an organization without adding value from the customers' perspective. Of the two categories of non-value-added time, NVAT1 is time required for the value-adding process steps (e.g., final inspections, operator training, facilities maintenance, and employee payroll management) to work. The improvement goal for such work is to minimize the time it takes and improve its quality so that it is done right the first time.

- **Non-value-added time (2) (NVAT2).** This term refers to the second category of non-value-added time, which is time not required for the value-adding process steps to work. The improvement goal is to eliminate all such unnecessary activities.

- **Process productivity (RTY).** The result of work that is done right the first time (i.e., there is a probability of zero defects in the throughput). Productivity is maximized when there are no defects scrapped or rework required in the output that is produced.

- **Defects per million opportunities (DPMO).** The number of defects observed in a million opportunities for producing the given defect. Defect sequences that are conditional on the occurrence of an initial defect are considered together as a single defect opportunity.

- **Process capability (Cp).** An indicator of the potential performance capability of a centered or ideal process as indicated by a comparison of the voice of the customer (i.e., what the customer wants) to the voice of the process (i.e., what the process is able to provide). It is measured as the ratio of specification tolerance width to six standard deviations in process variation as indicated using short-term data.

- **Process capability (Cpk).** An indicator of the actual performance capability that a process achieves, taking into account the real-world result of the process performance. It is measured as the minimum of the difference between the process average and the distance to the upper and lower specification limits divided by three standard deviations in process variation using short-term data.

- **Process sigma (short-term).** A standard deviation of a process parameter based on a short-term data sampling.

- **Process sigma (long-term).** A standard deviation of a process parameter based on a long-term data sampling.

- **Cost of poor quality (COPQ).** The sum of the costs directly associated with problems (e.g., delinquencies, defects, and delays) discovered internally or externally. This includes the direct costs of failures as well as the costs associated with correcting them.

In a Six Sigma measurement system, measures are taken of both product and process dimensions. These measures come together in the RTY, which involves using the product to check the process performance. The following table allocates the Six Sigma measures to either the product or the process, or both:

Six Sigma Measures

Product Measures	Process Measures	Combined Measures
DPMO (Production View)	Process Sigma (Short-Term)	RTY
DPU (Customers' View)	Process Sigma (Long-Term)	COPQ
	Cp	
	Cpk	
	Cycle-Time Measures	

The Six Sigma Recognize step focuses its analysis on the dimensions of business that achieve competitive advantage, win long-term customer loyalty, yield dedicated employees motivated to serve customers, and deliver expected return to investors. Strategic alignment follows when these top-tier measures are cascaded into the structure and language of the work processes so that all employees understand how they contribute to the desired results. Unfortunately, many organizational performance indicators provide business metrics that indicate only a general direction; this makes it difficult for an organization to understand what specific actions must be done at the process level to achieve the desired business results.

How does a company design a measurement system?

Process measurement requires time and costs money, so it must be done in a deliberate step-by-step manner so deep insight can be obtained into process performance and the benefits of measurement outweigh the costs of collecting data. Good measurements illuminate the inner operations of work processes and help management resolve problems quickly. They are sensitive enough to capture changes in the activities that produce the outcome of a business system. They are also timely; data-collection and measurement-analysis procedures should result in minimal decision delays.

It is important for an organization to know what it measures and why, as well as how good those measurements are for supporting decision making. The first step in design ing an organization-wide business-measurement system is to evaluate the status of the current measurements being used. By asking the questions in the self-assessment below, management can evaluate the effectiveness of its organization's current measurement system.

❑ What do we need to know?

❑ What measure will provide this knowledge?

❑ What does this measure enable us to do?

❑ How can this information be presented for a clear decision?

❑ What analysis method will deliver this type of information?

❑ What type of data is required to use this analysis method?

❑ Where is this type of data available?

If there are no clear answers to these questions, management must reconsider the measurements being used and the organization's approach to gaining understanding about its processes.

After determining what data should be monitored and why, an organization must map the cross-functional processes that deliver desirable results so it can determine their control points. Third, it must identify the critical tasks and capabilities required to keep the process operating within the performance envelope required by customers. Fourth, it must define the measures that track these tasks and capabilities.

What are measurement control points?

A measurement system must align with the flow of work processes so that it can detect changes in the activities that produce the outcome of the business system. Thus, it is essential to take measurements at points that give management the greatest opportunity to make decisions that support process adjustment and business control. The places at which critical measurement observations are taken are called *control points*. They represent places in a business or work process where (1) a "red flag" is raised when a process is in trouble (as indicated by the observed measure) and (2) operators can make adjustments to bring the process back into a controlled operating state. A measurement control point has the following characteristics:

❏ It is either a physical location or a point in time in a work process where control can be exercised over the quality or quantity of the throughput.

❏ It is used to monitor the progress of a work process and includes an assessment of the quality of the output from the prior process step as a "check" of process performance.

❏ It can be used to regulate the flow of work through a process and to balance the workload to ensure predictable work output.

❏ If it is a process bottleneck, it can be used to evaluate the capability of the entire production process to produce the desired level of output.

❏ It can be used to evaluate proposals for resource allocation to determine whether the process needs more support to perform at the desired level.

❏ It represents a good point for the management team to determine progress made during work processes.

To ensure that a measurement system is efficient, effective, and economical, two major types of concerns must be considered: structural and behavioral. Both are described below.

Structural considerations

Errors of index. In an attempt to explain complex performance, organizations sometimes lump together several measures to form a composite index. An example is combining customer satisfaction, average outgoing defects, and complaint levels into a "customer performance index." But such an index does not identify problems that might exist with a process's individual factors. For example, one factor might offset another, they might be sensitive to different response scales or time domains, or the effect of one might mask the other. As a result, such an index requires interpretation of the index itself, and the measure is not directly actionable.

Tyranny of the mean. Average performance is often presented in graphical form to indicate a performance trend over time. For example, customer satisfaction is usually presented as an average. This type of presentation can cause major problems in interpretation of the data; the truth about performance is found in individual observations that show the variance. Data should always be presented so that a spread or variance can be interpreted, even when an average is given to show a central tendency in the trend of the data over time.

Confounding of data. This occurs when a measurement system is not truly discrete in what it measures, and the measurements are not mutually exclusive and exhaustive. Because of this overlap, a measure of variable A also includes a part of variable B, producing the AB interaction; it also includes a part of variable C, producing the AC interaction, as well as a three-way ABC interaction. As a result, the level of variable A might not be what drives the results; it might be the interaction effects among the variables, which the measurements do not explicitly address.

Attribute data. To simplify information flow, decision filters are often used to collapse variable-measurement data into attribute performance categories. For example, all observations might be forced to fit into a five-point grading scale. This limits the type and sophistication of any data analysis that is done later. Analysis of attribute data is not as informative as analysis of measurement data. Once a conversion occurs, it is difficult to reverse the process because information is collapsed into broad categories.

Percentage information. Information is frequently presented as a percentage of the whole (e.g., a production line is said to have a "97% yield"). But this presents two problems. First, the scale that describes performance might not be good enough. With consumer products that are produced by the million on a weekly basis, a percentage scale will mask many errors that consumers will discover and believe to be significant. Second, a percentage scale often leads to "1% thinking": If a problem pertains to just 1% of the product, it might be viewed as too costly to fix, and corrective action might be put off.

Graphical presentations. Some graphical images have problems with the scale used for display, the time period that is illustrated, or the type of graphical image used for the data. Bar charts or pie charts are often used inappropriately to express information. Report graphics should always be clear and easy to interpret. Graphical images should be highlighted with text to aid in their interpretation and to ensure clarity of communication.

Traffic signals. Some measurement systems are simplified so much that the output is a "traffic signal," or a red/yellow/green indicator that shows whether a metric is on track. Although this type of measurement system permits quick assessment by management, it presents two problems. First, it does not indicate the shades of green or yellow variation that might exist. Second, the system is susceptible to manipulation by unscrupulous employees. A color assignment represents a subjective call, and there is little way to objectively evaluate the correctness of a color assignment without digging deeply into the underlying data.

Behavioral Considerations

Hidden criteria distort true performance. Hidden factors (e.g., safety stock levels, reorder points, transportation tables, and lead times) are often involved in decision making. These criteria can distort the true performance of a business system. An example is the use of internal transfer pricing to establish return to "internal P&L centers": To ensure that a profit is "appropriately allocated," information is distorted to divide the spoils according to the pecking order of internal power.

Measures might not reflect front-line activities. Measures might not represent the way employees are held accountable for their work. For instance, the measure of "customer satisfaction" does not cascade well through an organization unless it is broken down into specific causes of customer dissatisfaction, which are components that front-line workers can correct. The same is true for other macro-level measures, such as "productivity" and "employee satisfaction."

Measures might not include customer or market value. When designing a measurement system, it is easy to be internally focused. But keeping an external perspective provides objectivity about an organization's performance. Measurement systems should be anchored in the requirements of the customer. With no direct linkage to an external perspective, an organization can improve from an internal view yet totally miss the mark regarding customer-value delivery.

Old measures might not drive new strategy. An organization's management team might choose a strategic direction that significantly differs from those of the past. When this happens, the old set of performance measures might not capture all the nuances in the change process or provide a good indication of the progress being made toward achieving the new objectives.

Operational performance might not deliver the right measures. An organization's routine way of working might lack connectivity to a strategy-based measurement system. For instance, if an organization makes "time to market" a critical measure of performance, then its work processes must measure all sub-components of the time equation. If work processes do not capture the components of the measurement desired, it is impossible to accurately portray the process's overall performance. For a measurement system to deliver Six Sigma results, it must have connectivity from top to bottom *and* from bottom to top.

▶ TIP

A process-performance measurement system must meet the following design criteria to be a best-practice daily management system capable of managing a Six Sigma business.

– Measures must be actionable. Managers must be able to interpret what to do as a result of the indicated performance.

– Measures must be auditable. Performance should be capable of evaluation by a third party who obtains the same results, thus leading to a consistent operational decision.

– Measures must be standardized across operating units. All work areas that perform the same functions should use the same measures. This facilitates internal comparisons.

- Measures must be reliable and indicate desired results. Measured data must reflect actual performance and should be predictive of the outcome of the process.
- Measures must be timely indicators of performance. They should permit corrective action to be taken quickly when observations show the need to adjust a work process.
- Measures must be capable of validation against external systems. Measurements that are meaningful only inside an organization are not optimal for facilitating benchmarks against external work processes. Wherever possible, generic measurements (e.g., quality, cost, and time) should be used to permit easy comparisons in determining best practices.
- Measures must be related to defects, cost, and cycle time. These three building blocks of process productivity should be used for measuring all work transactions, for calculating process-sigma levels, and for establishing work-process productivity-improvement targets.
- Measures must be owned by process managers and team members. The people who are held responsible for the work should be accountable for its results. They must believe that the measures are fair and appropriate and that they own the process performance, and they must use these measures to take improvement action when necessary.
- Measures must be predictive of final results. In-process measures that are part of the measurement system must be highly correlated and causative of the results of process performance.
- Measures must reflect the expectations of all stakeholders. They must mirror the viewpoint of customers, have utility for process management, and deliver shareholders' expectations.

Developing a line-of-sight measurement system

A Six Sigma measurement system is capable of tracking performance from the business Y's (i.e., the top-tier metrics of business success) to the process X's (i.e., the front-line measures of process performance), as well as tracking performance contributions from the process X's to the business Y's. In such a system, business success is evaluated daily as work processes are managed. Local managers measure progress at control points and can adapt the process parameters to optimize cycle time, reduce defects, and maintain the lowest possible cost while optimizing the entire organization's throughput.

To do this successfully, the organization must determine how its front-line work processes deliver desired levels of performance. This is done by developing a *line of sight*—a linked and aligned performance-relationship structure. (See Question 12 for a related discussion of $y = f(x)$ MECE logic.) A line of sight enables executives to see how front-line workers deliver the company strategy, and it permits front-line workers to understand how their activities deliver the company strategy. To achieve this connectivity, performance measures must be linked by a chain of objectives that integrate the organization's actions to deliver predictable outcomes. In addition, work-process teams manage a coherent set of coordinated actions that deliver the customers' needs on a profitable and sustainable basis. Process measures, cost measures, and customer measures must all be integrated at the front-line level using a work-process scorecard (see Question 43).

Balanced scorecard measurement systems

The balanced scorecard, created by Robert S. Kaplan and David P. Norton of the Harvard Graduate School of Business, gives managers comprehensive insight into business performance at a glance. It supplements the financial measures of an organization's performance with operational measures that illuminate performance according to the perspectives of all business stakeholders (i.e., customers, employees, managers, and shareholders). Typically a scorecard is developed to let senior managers see all key performance indicators together in one place. The following characteristics are typical of balanced scorecards:

❏ They provide a completely detailed log of performance.

❏ They are kept by workers who are dedicated to recording data and who do not actively participate in the work processes.

❏ Neither the data recorders nor the scorecard is consulted for advice when work processes are performed.

❏ Scorecards are provided to managers after work is performed to evaluate improvement opportunities for the future.

The following design features distinguish a Six Sigma performance-measurement system from a balanced scorecard system.

❏ A Six Sigma approach to measurement applies the function $y = f(x)$ to break down work-process activities and ensure that measures are statistically connected with business activities at control points of the process.

❏ Measurements are always linked to the customer. This illustrates how critical-to-satisfaction (CTS) issues are embedded in the work processes as critical-to-quality (CTQ) factors.

❏ Customer requirements for performance are embedded in results expectations and become reference points for measuring achievements.

❏ Causality is determined using statistical inferences to characterize what quantitative relationships exist among in-process results measures.

❏ Response to performance concerns is based on analysis aimed at the reduction of both special-cause and common-cause variation. Special-cause variation is due to fine-tuning of process features; common-cause variation is due to management assumptions or the design of the process.

Scorecards provide a detailed report that is useful for an after-the-fact analysis of events, but they do not provide a good role model for routine business operations and decisions, and they fail to provide the action orientation needed for daily management. In addition, a scorecard can seem like a smorgasbord of measurement. Neither the connectivity of one measure to another nor the linkage from one tier of management to the next is required.

As a result, the balanced scorecard is not a Six Sigma measurement system. Organizations using a balanced scorecard end up adapting measures that seem right but do not have a causal impact for improving business results. Using a customer dashboard is a better approach.

Customer dashboard measurement systems

A Six Sigma customer dashboard measurement system works much like an airplane pilot's cockpit. A heads-up display in front of the pilot has the most important indicators to ensure safety of flight. These measurements are placed where the pilot cannot ignore them, so he/she is likely to take appropriate action. When the display illustrates that something is wrong with a key mission indicator, the pilot turns to a secondary set of much more numerous measurement systems on the overhead panel to diagnose the problem and determine the appropriate action to take. For factors that are not mission critical, there is a third location: behind the pilot's back on a panel of circuit beakers.

The following characteristics of a customer dashboard system do not necessarily hold true for a balanced scorecard.

❏ The measurement process is based on variation. Good processes will have less variation for critical measurement parameters than poor processes. To improve a process, management must reduce the variation in the process that is due to *common cause*—the natural variation designed into core process activities.

❏ Connectivity among performance indicators is based on statistical analysis that demonstrates causality, not on groupings of measures that appear to influence each other.

❏ Process ownership is established for implementing the process-measurement system and for monitoring the measures to achieve desired results.

❏ Accountability for performance is a requirement of process ownership. No excuses for performance shortfalls or over-achievements are permitted. Any unexpected performance, good or bad, must be understood and explained.

Starting a customer dashboard design project

The following sequence of activities make up the step-by-step process for creating a customer dashboard.

1. Set the direction. Determine the value proposition for the mainstream business.

2. Determine the context. Establish a competitive market proposition for the entire business.

3. Map the enterprise. Analyze how the essential business and work-process actions are integrated with the measurement system.

4. Identify critical business-control points. Map the enterprise and determine where the critical business-control points are located. This is one of the most important tasks in building a customer dashboard. Without knowledge of the mechanism by which the control can be exercised and determining the degree of effectiveness that can be directed at that point, it is impossible to make any pragmatic application of an observed control point.

5. Delegate responsibility for processes and measures. Delegate authority for control of key measurement control-point decisions to process owners. (See the Tip at the end of Question 5 for details about holding people accountable for the quality of their work.)

6. Calculate the measurement baseline for current performance. Find benchmarks in external organizations that challenge management to strive for business excellence.

Three aspects must be well managed to result in a workable customer dashboard: building an enterprise model, building a measurement map, and determining accountability for work-process performance. These aspects are outlined below.

Building an enterprise model

The following sequence of steps is a basis for building an enterprise model.

1. Model the key organizational business processes as a high-level flow diagram to illustrate what the organization does and how it gets done.

2. Identify the perspectives of key customers and stakeholders in the organization. Determine what is important (i.e., critical to quality, or CTQ) about the organization's output from each of their viewpoints. These aspects become items that are critical to satisfaction (CTS) for the organization. This translation of a customer's CTQ into a CTS for an organization follows an approach similar to that of the translation of Y's into component X's using the relationship of $y = f(x)$.

3. Translate the high-level flow diagram created in step 1 into a series of deployment maps to show how collaboration occurs in delivering performance results. Organize deployment maps into "centers of excellence" or "communities of practice." A center of excellence is a core business process that conducts key repetitive tasks on behalf of customers. Examples are production and distribution. A community of practice is a functional organization that supports the core business processes but performs a task essential only for the mainstream processes to operate smoothly. Examples are purchasing, human resources, and information systems.

4. Divide each deployment map into a set of thought maps that define the relationship of the CTS factors to the organization's CTQ measures at this level of process detail.

5. Develop a decision-rights matrix to summarize how each involved person participates in key decisions and to determine how accountability and responsibility are allocated for each decision.

6. Validate the measurement system's functionality by conducting a process audit.

7. Carry forward all learning into the creation of a measurement specification that defines all the critical ingredients of each customer dashboard measure.

8. Apply the measurement system in the strategic planning process, regular management reports, and work-performance analysis.

Once an enterprise model is built, the management team must establish how it will use the measurement control points to manage business performance. This requires specification of the measurement system via a measurement map.

Building a measurement map

The process for building a measurement map links the business Y's (i.e., shareholder value and brand value) to the process X's (i.e., quality, cost, and time) using $y = f(x)$ analysis. This analysis consists of stratification of the top-level business measures into their component work-process measures so that they are mutually exclusive and completely exhaustive within each measurement tree. Several trees can exist concurrently to represent *confounding*, or interactions among variables that are evaluated together. This occurs among the three major branches of quality, cost, and time. The sequence of steps for building a measurement map is as follows:

1. Establish management measurements for top-level business Y's.

2. Assess the current state of the measurement system and its linkage to business Y's.

3. Accumulate process X's into intermediate Y's (explained below) to deliver business Y's.

4. Operationally define all key measurements and all opportunities for defects.

5. Determine the sources of variation for process X's.

6. Identify management-controllable factors for each X measure.

7. Select the sampling methods and frequency of reporting for X's.

8. Create the graphical methods for presentation and interpretation of X's.

9. Assign accountability for the performance of X's, intermediate Y's, and business Y's.

10. Choose owners for business Y's to ensure implementation compliance.

11. Document the measurement specification for each business Y.

12. Assign managerial oversight for the entire business.

13. Align business-decision processes to the measurement system.

14. Reduce work complexity that adds variation without increasing customer value.

15. Apply the measurement system to streamline value-added work.

16. Implement the measurement system.

The intermediate Y's referenced above are similar to a balanced scorecard. One set of intermediate Y's includes the indicators listed below. Unlike a balanced scorecard, however, all these indicators are linked together using a $y = f(x)$ analysis.

❑ System-delivery flexibility: delivery of the maximum production volume to meet market requirements and customer demand.

❑ Delivery to promise: accuracy of delivery in accordance with promises made to customers.

❑ Profit maximization: production of the maximum profit capability from the contributions of capital investments and operational work processes.

❑ First-time quality: the rolled throughput yield (RTY) of business, which demonstrates ability to deliver quality results without losing productivity due to poor quality.

Managing work using a customer dashboard

The final aspect of deploying a customer dashboard is to use it for managing the daily work and routine operations of a business. During the execution of any business-improvement plan, management must perform two distinct activities: evaluate the quality of the work being done and steward the organization's resources to achieve performance targets.

Managers must distinguish between two types of objectives: (1) those that define the organization's approach to business improvement and evaluate the completeness of its deployment and (2) those that evaluate achievement using the measures of business results to ensure stewardship and recognize accountability. Self-assessment methods should separate the evaluation of plans and their deployment from the results achieved. Not only are these two activities distinct, but they are usually separated in time and in responsibility for performance.

Process monitoring involves continually sampling work-process performance to determine how well a process is operating over time. As long as it operates within its desirable performance envelope, it is considered to be in a state of control. When it exceeds these boundary conditions, it is considered a rogue process that requires variation management.

The purpose of process monitoring is not to evaluate how good a process is performing; it is to capture early indicators of performance shifts that can lead to less-than-desirable performance. This is one of the most important benefits of implementing a customer dashboard measurement system. Such a system enables business leaders to detect and stay ahead of emerging problems.

Customer dashboards provide a balanced, real-time, customer-focused, action-oriented approach for the objective management of business and work processes. Their only drawback is the difficulty of putting these measurement systems into place, which requires cross-functional efforts on behalf of the management team. Even more important, the daily use and operation of customer dashboards must become the core of an organization's way of working. Managing via a customer dashboard requires disciplined application and thorough follow-up using Six Sigma tools and analysis methods to determine and eliminate the root cause of critical business problems.

If members of a management team do not focus on diagnosing common-cause performance issues, they nullify their responsibility as effective business leaders. When senior management takes the lead in the investigation of special-cause variation and assigning the cause—or blame—for the problem, it undermines the organizational structure by not holding process owners accountable for their performance results.

The use of a customer dashboard assures an organization's business leaders that management's objective for process information is satisfied, but not at the expense of process owners' loss of stewardship for resources. Customer dashboards are intended for use by all involved workers. Self-management continues to be the best principle for process operations.

Deploying a measurement system

The manner in which a measurement system is built and deployed determines whether the organization ultimately accepts or rejects it. When it is built collaboratively, an atmosphere of acceptance is created because members of the organization help design it and understand the rationale behind its components. The following activities help to ensure company-wide acceptance of a measurement system:

❑ Use of a workshop format for creation of the enterprise model and the measurement map builds acceptance and establishes credibility among middle managers.

❑ Active participation of all affected process owners in defining the measurement specifications ensures that they will apply the results.

❑ Cascading the measurement system by business-process area and across functional groups ensures integration of the measurement system into the fabric of work activities.

❑ Embedding the measurement system into the information-management system ensures compliance with structured measurement by eliminating the opportunity for calculation errors and "creative interpretation" of measurement definitions.

How is Six Sigma performance sustained?

Long-term maintenance of the efforts of a Six Sigma initiative requires the full engagement of an organization's business system. The five components of such a system, listed below, are united through leadership exercised at all levels of the organization's infrastructure.

1. The organization's mission, or purpose.

2. Its vision, or strategic direction.

3. Its strategy, or action plan for achieving its vision.

4. Its culture, or way of working that unites employees into a common bond and motivates their continued dedication to the purpose.

5. The set of systems that support this infrastructure, including human resources, management information systems, and quality systems.

Six Sigma fundamentally changes the way organizations work in the following ways:

❑ Employees communicate using data—rather than theories, opinions, wishes, hopes, or desires—to express principles about business operations.

❑ The organization focuses on consistency of process and constancy of purpose; intolerance for variation is encouraged.

❑ The organization shifts from measuring only results to also measuring inputs and in-process performance in an effort to better understand why certain results are achieved.

❑ Measurement is required, and accountability for performance is encouraged.

❑ Managers own their work processes and take responsibility for managing their control systems for inputs as well as their in-process work in an effort to satisfy customers.

❑ A solution resolves a problem permanently rather than acting as a short-term fix that allows the problem to eventually return.

❑ Employees seek to satisfy customers throughout the organization's relationship with them. This builds customer loyalty and increases the organization's brand value in the market.

- Expectations for suppliers elevate as they conform to the Six Sigma requirements for making quality contributions to the organization's business system.

- Learning occurs across the entire organization, which increases the acceptance of improvement ideas demonstrated through Six Sigma projects.

- Collaboration becomes a standard operating procedure as the organization focuses on working as a team to serve its customers and outperform its competitors.

The secret of sustaining Six Sigma is for an organization to adopt these methods as a part of its core business and make them just as important as valuing customers or striving for innovation in their products and/or services. An organization can take the following actions to ensure that Six Sigma performance is sustained.

- **Build commitment among business leaders.** Commitment goes beyond participation ("I was there"), buy-in ("I agree"), and involvement ("I did this"); it is the highest degree of participative leadership. A leadership team's members must accept the Six Sigma methodology and serve as executive sponsors by establishing a vision of flawless execution and promoting the use of Six Sigma methods in all areas of the organization.

- **Integrate Six Sigma into the strategic-planning process.** An organization must link all improvement projects directly to the change strategies of the senior leadership team. This accelerates achievement of business goals and helps align the organization's efforts so it focuses on the most important changes from a long-term strategic perspective. This alignment requires an organization to have a line of sight from the business strategies to the tactics that implement them. Employees at the work-process level must see how their daily work contributes to achievement of the strategic objectives.

- **Integrate customer-relationship management with Six Sigma.** An organization must maintain active listening posts that allow it to hear the voice of the customer and respond to customer concerns in real time. Six Sigma requires that critical-to-satisfaction (CTS) customer requirements be measurable so their baseline performance can be improved.

- **Design work as a business process and organize it with an enterprise model.** An enterprise model is a fundamental requirement for building a business-measurement system and is key to applying customer focus across an organization. Processes must be organized for "concept-to-customer" delivery of results, beginning with solicitation of customer input regarding design requirements and ending with the delivery of finished goods or services to the customer. Each process has an owner who is accountable to the organization for the delivery of that process's contribution to business results.

- **Implement the Six Sigma measurement system.** After appropriate performance indicators are developed, a line-of-sight measurement system can operate effectively (see Question 44) and process management can be used. Quantifiable measures must be developed and tested to determine their connection to business-results measures. Can a predictive approach be used based on the business Y's and process X's? Once statistical inference has been demonstrated and causality proven, all process owners should be held accountable for using the measurement approach as a control function for their daily process management.

❑ **Develop feedback and incentive systems.** For a Six Sigma initiative to be sustained over a long period of time, employees must feel good about the strategic value of their work (see Question 5). Feedback systems allow for the results of Six Sigma projects to be shared across an organization. This enables the extension of a project to multiple areas of the organization. Peer recognition for work done in a Six Sigma project provides a strong incentive. Companies implementing Six Sigma must devise reward systems that are fair and equitable to all parties involved in a project (see Question 42).

❑ **Provide the resources required to ensure success.** The basic formula for success in a Six Sigma initiative is to take the right people (Black Belts), assign them the right projects (those that have strategic value to the organization), deploy the right methods and tools (the DMAIC and DMADV approaches), and thereby derive the desired results. The executive sponsor and business leaders determine the ultimate success of an initiative by striving to dedicate resources in a way that delivers the best results for the organization. For management to obtain desired results, it must maintain high standards while selecting Black Belts and make this position a true career-growth opportunity for those who serve. Projects must be selected with care to ensure that the organization achieves the benefits it needs most.

How does a company plan Six Sigma for enduring success?

An organization's business leaders must develop an action plan to sustain an initial Six Sigma effort. For Six Sigma to become an enduring initiative, three areas require development: support infrastructure, strategic focus, and outreach efforts.

Support infrastructure. To make Six Sigma a lasting influence on the way an organization operates, the organization must make Six Sigma part of its mainstream infrastructure rather than a stand-alone special effort. This transition of a change initiative to a mainstream activity is sometimes called "institutionalization." Deployment of a Six Sigma initiative requires support from the organization and reinforcement from its leadership team. The following support services should be created to encourage Black Belts and improvement teams and to mainstream Six Sigma into an organization:

❑ Development networks for Black Belts and Master Black Belts.

❑ Best-practice sharing through a variety of methods, including the company newsletter and intranet, as well as an annual Six Sigma conference to showcase the best projects.

❑ Integration of Six Sigma awareness and skills training into the organization's employee-development programs, ranging from new-employee orientation, to the initial management development program for front-line supervisors, to advanced leadership-development programs for business leaders.

❑ Inclusion of Six Sigma in the organization's strategic-planning and personnel-evaluation processes, promotion criteria, and rewards and recognition program.

❑ Integration of Six Sigma with existing quality systems (e.g., ISO 9000).

Strategic focus. A second ingredient for ensuring long-term success is to use Six Sigma to stimulate growth opportunities—through merger and acquisition, new product development, or expanding the organization's business model into new areas. As an organization matures in its ability to use Six Sigma methods for business improvement, the emphasis shifts from projects scoped for training to those with a more strategic significance for the organization. For example, for an organization's first few projects, Black Belts focus predominantly on improving the organization's operational and business work processes. For later projects, Black Belts shift their efforts to systems integration and strategic alignment by tackling projects that integrate work processes into business systems. (See Question 50 for ideas for strategic Six Sigma projects.)

Outreach efforts. A third ingredient for ensuring long-term success is for an organization to extend its internal Six Sigma efforts to include suppliers in the problem-solving process (see Question 48) and to dedicate Six Sigma resources to work with targeted customers to improve their ability to use the organization's products and services (see Question 49). These outreach efforts seek to build partnerships with external entities that have strategic significance for the long-term viability of a business. When these external entities become collaborators in business and employ similar problem-solving and design techniques, the entire organization can operate as a system to resolve issues and design its future.

What is a Six Sigma
implementation audit?

An organization can use a Six Sigma implementation audit as frequently as necessary to assess the quality of progress made to date on its Six Sigma initiative. Some organizations find that conducting such audits is a good way to encourage their individual business units to follow the standard deployment plan. An implementation audit typically evaluates management performance by asking questions such as the following:

1. What is the vision for deployment of Six Sigma in your business unit? How broad an application of the Six Sigma initiative is planned? Is it limited in scope to operations or production processes, or is it deployed to all business and support processes?

2. How does Six Sigma support your business unit's goals? Do business leaders clearly communicate the linkage between Six Sigma and their business unit's goals?

3. What actions have business leaders taken to demonstrate their sponsorship and committed support of the Six Sigma initiative? Are regular meetings held with project champions, process owners, Black Belts, and Master Black Belts? Are updates on the progress of the Six Sigma initiative included in regular staff meetings and employee communications?

4. Have business leaders taken any specific steps to include Six Sigma targets in process owners' performance objectives to establish process owners' accountability for delivering improvement-project benefits?

5. How are Black Belts selected? Does the selection process nominate high-potential people for open positions? Does the procedure follow standard practices for nomination and selection of Black Belts?

6. How are Black Belt projects selected? How can you ensure that Black Belts are working on those projects that have the greatest impact for organizational improvement?

7. What process measures have been established? How do they relate to the business Y's of the organization? Are there plans to develop a Six Sigma customer dashboard and monitor these measurements through the organization's information system?

8. What orientation is given to business leaders who are not project champions or process owners to help them understand Six Sigma and its implications for

the way the organization will be managed? Is this orientation effective in eliciting support from these individuals when it is needed for a Six Sigma project?

9. What channels are used to communicate to all employees about Six Sigma? Which of these communication channels have been the most effective?

10. What forms of reward and recognition have been used to support Six Sigma in your business unit? Do all employee groups believe this system is fair and adequate?

11. Do key business processes have either multiple process owners or cross-functional business leaders? If so, how has Six Sigma been adopted by these process or business areas?

12. Have you experienced any unique complexities or applications in the implementation of Six Sigma in your business unit?

How do I do it?

An implementation audit is planned like any other audit. The team conducting the audit must first be identified and then trained in the auditing process. A standard questionnaire should be used to query members of the organization and collect information about the progress in implementation. A quick review of results is conducted on-site after the completion of the audit. This is followed by a more detailed final report that describes areas of strength and opportunities for process improvement, as well as specific recommendations. The Six Sigma leadership committee should review the report and take responsibility for defining the priority improvements and implementing any required corrective action.

How does a company extend Six Sigma to its suppliers?

Perhaps the most natural way for an organization to externally extend its Six Sigma program is to include its suppliers in the initiative. After all, suppliers influence the performance of an organization's key process input variables (KIPIVs), which eventually become process X's. To get these variables under control, the processes that produce these inputs to an organization's internal work processes must come under the same degree of control as the organization's own processes.

What steps should an organization take to extend Six Sigma to its suppliers? Integration of an organization's global supply chain into a Six Sigma system requires resources, dedication of a small staff of experienced Master Black Belts and Black Belts, and the commitment of the organization's supply-chain managers to developing strategic alliances with suppliers. Many organizations take a cost-neutral approach to the inclusion of suppliers in a Six Sigma program by either charging for training or taking cost reductions in materials or services based on savings gained through subsequent projects. Others take the approach that all savings are returned on training projects because these projects are selected to improve the parts or services that the supplier provides to the organization. Whichever approach an organization takes, it must be applied uniformly to all suppliers, with the recognition that the benefit should be mutual to both the organization and the suppliers.

While some organizations use an abbreviated program to train suppliers—similar to a Green Belt level of proficiency—the analytical value of a Six Sigma initiative is not fully transferred. It is best to train at least two people in each supplier organization, one as a project champion (see Question 14) and the other as a Black Belt. This way, the organization can benefit from the suppliers' improved managerial knowledge and the analytical skills imparted to their Black Belts. A small supplier would not require a full-time Black Belt, as the number of exceptionally involved problems might be limited.

In designing a program for suppliers, an organization must focus on their needs. Most large manufacturing companies have their own Six Sigma programs, so it is not necessary to focus on them. Instead, an organization should focus on small- to medium-size suppliers that work on custom parts or have unique processes. These companies have the most to gain by implementing Six Sigma. Suppliers with the worst record for an organization's critical product-related process X's should be the organization's initial focus point.

Finally, to organize its supplier-related activities, an organization should develop a Six Sigma implementation plan for suppliers using the same approach it used for its own deployment plan (see Question 19).

QUESTION 49

How does a company extend Six Sigma to its customers?

Just as it is natural for an organization to extend Six Sigma to its suppliers, it is equally natural for it to do the same with its customers. This additional service differentiates an organization's relationship with its customers from the relationships those customers have with competing organizations.

The first step an organization should take to extend Six Sigma to customers is to involve them in projects that require their input. This way, the organization can more clearly define their expectations. A logical extension of this is for the organization to report on the progress made in these projects, so customers understand the benefits they are deriving from cooperating with the company's Six Sigma teams. The second step in engaging customers is to form joint teams to work on eliminating shared problem areas. The third step is to involve customers in creating the design specification for DMADV projects that will deliver an organization's future products or services. During these steps, it is essential that customers always see a clear value proposition in return for their involvement.

To supplement these activities, an organization can develop a customer-focused Six Sigma effort to improve the quality of its customer-relationship-management (CRM) systems. CRM improvement includes account management (i.e., setup of customer account information so that it contains no errors and is updated frequently and accurately) and management of customer contacts so a company does not overwhelm its customers with too many calls.

Another possibility is for an organization to invite its customers to send Black Belt candidates to attend its internal Six Sigma training program. Such mutual involvement in supporting customers' improvement efforts can lead to "most favored supplier" status in recognition of the excellence with which an organization conducts business with its customers. Whenever Six Sigma achieves such a competitive advantage, the organizational payback can be significant over the long term.

Why integrate Six Sigma into everything?

To outpace its competitors, an organization must effectively integrate its global business operations and focus on its key customers. These customers' requirements typically become more rigorous with time, which requires a thoughtful, objective response that enables an organization to maintain market leadership. An organization seeking to respond globally to its competition must establish a common culture—with communal work practices, standardized analytical tools, and mutual respect for cultural differences—across the organization.

Six Sigma can facilitate an organization's global competitiveness. If maintaining a long-term view and creating an enduring competitive difference are important for an organization, its management team should consider sponsoring Six Sigma improvement projects in the following areas:

❑ **Mergers and acquisitions.** Preparation for a merger or acquisition requires a thorough investigation of the targeted organization. This includes considering the value of its assets; focusing on its current operating processes, the potential for savings, and increasing revenue; and improving its level of efficiency regarding capital assets. An acquiring firm can use Six Sigma–trained Black Belts to determine the magnitude of the targeted organization's hidden factory and to estimate the cost of poor quality, which can be remedied with improvement projects once the acquisition is completed. In this way, part of the purchase price can be returned in the form of a more efficient and effective workplace.

❑ **E-business planning.** The Internet provides an easy way for an organization to move into a new market or distribution channel to expand its business and access new markets for its products and services. To build a competitive position in the e-commerce arena, an organization must effectively plan its e-business growth, taking the same steps for e-business planning that it would take for normal business-plan development. These steps include implementation of the Six Sigma Recognize step for the e-business model it intends to develop (i.e., a business process design) in which the emphasis is on e-marketing and sales with follow-up fulfillment of the orders.

❑ **New product development.** Organizational growth resulting from extending product lines and creating new customers is the key to a sustainable future. Such growth is possible only when an organization incorporates new technologies into its new products and services, sells new products into old markets, and sells existing products into new markets. A Six Sigma project in this area focuses on ensuring that an organization's product-development division provides a continuous stream of new and innovative products to the marketplace based on the expectations of external customers. Design for Six Sigma provides the toolkit and processes to deliver flawless new products that exceed customer performance expectations without exceeding their price expectations.

❏ **Risk management.** A Six Sigma company must develop a better way to manage business risks than setting aside surplus funds or purchasing insurance. Risk management has two viewpoints: one that looks at risks as things gone wrong, and one that looks at managing business-development opportunities under conditions of risk. Business leaders know that there is no such thing as a risk-free investment; all growth has some degree of risk. Choosing alternative business-development opportunities in the face of different types and magnitudes of risk is the challenge facing management today. A Six Sigma project in this area focuses on quantifying risk and improving the way it is included in an organization's capital decision-making process.

❏ **National and global brand development.** The value of a brand lingers longer in customers' minds than their satisfaction with a single interaction with an organization. A brand has an image associated with a long-term commercial relationship. Senior management must work to develop the concept that an organization's brand is worthy of trust and is of enduring value long after the product has been consumed or the service has been rendered. A Six Sigma project in this area focuses on determining the relative effectiveness of advertising and other marketing tools for different communication channels regarding various aspects of a corporate brand, such as brand awareness and brand consideration.

❏ **Management of innovation and emerging technologies.** In new product development, innovation—developing new customer solutions for the most promising emerging technologies—is key. Doing so enables an organization to grow in a natural manner through the invention of new products. But how can an organization consistently offer great products to the market when there are so many technologies and potential applications from which to choose? A Six Sigma project in this area focuses on the way an organization's business leaders make decisions about investing in new products and the process for delivering new product concepts to consumers.

All the projects listed above can help improve an organization's enduring competitiveness. Any organization that hopes to compete successfully in the future must master the application of Six Sigma to improve its ability to work at optimal speed while achieving an extensive scale of application. Six Sigma practices and methods do more than support individual projects to improve parts of a business; they also drive success across the entire business-enterprise model and help an organization achieve a competitive advantage by facilitating breakthrough levels of performance. All this helps an organization align itself with the shifting demands of the global market.

ASQ Certified Six Sigma Black Belt
Body of Knowledge

The topics in this Body of Knowledge were initially developed by the American Society for Quality (ASQ) to define the knowledge base for Six Sigma Black Belts. This Body of Knowledge assists individuals in developing a study plan for certification as an ASQ Certified Six Sigma Black Belt (CSSBB). This information provides useful guidance for the ASQ Examination Development Committee as well as for candidates preparing to take the CSSBB examination. For additional information on the CSSBB examination and the Body of Knowledge, please visit the ASQ web site at www.asq.org.

Bibliography

Breyfogle, Forrest W., James M. Cupello, and Becki Meadows. 2000. *Managing Six Sigma.* Hoboken, NJ: John Wiley & Sons.

Eckes, George. 2002. *Six Sigma Team Dynamics.* Hoboken, NJ: John Wiley & Sons.

_____. 2001. *Making Six Sigma Last.* Hoboken, NJ: John Wiley & Sons.

_____. 2000. *The Six Sigma Revolution.* Hoboken, NJ: John Wiley & Sons.

Ehrlich, Betsi Harris. 2002. *Transactional Six Sigma and Lean Servicing.* New York: St. Lucie Press.

George, Michael L. 2002. *Lean Six Sigma.* New York: McGraw-Hill.

GOAL/QPC. 2002. *The Six Sigma Memory Jogger II.* Salem, NH: GOAL/QPC.

GOAL/QPC and Six Sigma Academy. 2002. *The Black Belt Memory Jogger.* Salem, NH: GOAL/QPC.

Harry, Mikel, and Richard Schroeder. 1999. *Six Sigma: The Breakthrough Management Strategy Revolutionizing the World's Top Corporations.* New York: Doubleday.

Pande, Peter S., Robert P. Neuman, and Roland R. Cavanagh. 2001. *The Six Sigma Way Team Fieldbook.* New York: McGraw-Hill.

_____. 2000. *The Six Sigma Way.* New York: McGraw-Hill.

Pande, Peter S., and Larry Holpp. 2001. *What Is Six Sigma?* New York: McGraw-Hill.

Smith, Dick, Jerry Blakeslee, and Richard Koonce. 2002. *Strategic Six Sigma.* Hoboken, NJ: John Wiley & Sons.

Snee, Ronald D., and Roger W. Hoerl. 2002. *Leading Six Sigma.* New York: Financial Times Prentice Hall.

_____. 2001. *Statistical Thinking: Improving Business Performance.* Pacific Grove, CA: Duxbury Press.

Ulrich, Dave, Steve Kerr, and Ron Ashkenas. 2002. *The GE Work-Out.* New York: McGraw-Hill.

Watson, Gregory H., ed. 2003. *Technical Foundations of Six Sigma*. Milwaukee: ASQ Quality Press.

Watson, Gregory H. 1994. *Business Systems Engineering*. Hoboken, NJ: John Wiley & Sons.

_____. 1993. *Strategic Benchmarking*. Hoboken, NJ: John Wiley & Sons.

Womack, James P., and Daniel T. Jones. 1996. *Lean Thinking*. New York: Simon & Schuster.

Glossary

activity-based costing (ABC)
Determining the actual cost of a product or service by tracing the cost back to the specific activities that produce or provide it.

Affinity Diagram
A method that enables a team to generate a large number of ideas and then organize natural groupings among them to understand the essence of a problem and identify solutions.

Analytic Hierarchy Process (AHP)
A decision-support tool that provides a logical approach for making a complex decision by enabling the decision-maker to determine trade-offs among options to find the most appropriate choice.

attribute
A characteristic that can have only one value (e.g., 0 or 1, green or red, go or no-go).

balanced scorecard
A measurement system based on gathering a comprehensive set of performance measures to enable an organization to determine its strengths and areas needing improvement.

baseline
A current or historical level of performance that is used as a standard of comparison for future performance improvements.

benchmarking
The practice of establishing performance targets and change projects based on how an organization's processes compare with the industry's best practices.

block diagram
A graphical linkage of blocks, which are labeled with noun-verb phrases, that indicates the logical sequence of a series of events. A block diagram is the elemental graphical form of a process model or flowchart.

brand value
The market's sustained confidence that a company can provide enduring customer satisfaction.

business process
An end-to-end sequence of activities that defines one or more business functions required to deliver goods or services to a customer. Processes serving external customers are considered core business processes; those serving internal customers are considered support services.

business-process improvement
The practice of flowcharting a process, accurately identifying customer needs, identifying non-productive work, and redesigning the process to better meet customer needs with less chance for errors and at a lower operating cost.

business Y
An output indicator of success in delivery of desired business results, such as shareholder value and brand value.

catchball
Give-and-take dialogue that occurs among organizational levels during negotiation and leads to shared objectives or consensus on direction in a policy-deployment-planning system.

Cause & Effect/Fishbone Diagram
A diagram that enables a team to identify, explore, and graphically display, in increasing detail, all possible causes of a problem in an effort to identify its root cause(s).

charter
A written commitment (or contract) by management that states the purpose and objectives of an improvement-project team. Resources, performance targets, participants, and review authority are specifically addressed.

confounding
A combined effect or statistical condition that occurs when two or more variables (or their interactions) are evaluated together so that the unique effects of each variable cannot be separated.

continuous improvement
A step-wise, incremental, continuous effort to improve performance of a process or sequential improvement in the performance of a product's features over time. The idea that management improvement is necessarily a continuous activity to ensure ongoing customer satisfaction and improved performance.

control chart
A graphical rendition of a characteristic's performance across time in relation to its natural limits and central tendency. It is used to evaluate whether a process is in a state of statistical control.

control point
A physical location or point in time in a work process at which critical measurement observations are taken and control can be exercised over the quality or quantity of the throughput.

core business process
A process that delivers a critical business outcome (i.e., a key driver to providing value to external customers).

cost of poor quality (COPQ)
The sum of costs incurred for efforts made to prevent and detect problems and to correct internal and external failures. COPQ is often offset by the *return on quality*, which is the benefit received from reductions in scrap, rework, and lost time, plus a productivity improvement from using the failure time to produce additional products.

Cp
An indicator of the potential performance capability of a centered or ideal process as indicated by a comparison of the voice of the customer (i.e., what the customer wants) to the voice of the process (i.e., what the process is able to provide). It is measured as the ratio of specification tolerance width to six standard deviations in process variation as indicated using short-term data.

Cpk
An indicator of the actual performance capability that a process achieves, taking into account the real-world result of the process performance. It is measured as the minimum

of the difference between the process average and the distance to the upper and lower specification limits divided by three standard deviations in process variation using short-term data.

critical to quality (CTQ)
Describes product or service characteristics that significantly influence one or more CTSes in terms of quality.

critical to satisfaction (CTS)
Describes characteristics that are critical to the way customers use, apply, or consume an organization's products or services.

customer dashboard
A measurement system based on connectivity among performance indicators based on causality, reducing variation to improve processes, and process ownership that includes accountability for performance.

customer focus
The concept that top priority must be given to working on factors that satisfy short- and long-term customer needs. All decisions must be made in full understanding of their impact on external customers. Some organizations also extend this principle to their internal customers.

cycle time
The total time required to successfully complete all the tasks that are required for a work process.

defects per million opportunities (DPMO)
A measure of quality that indicates the number of defects observed in a million opportunities for producing the given defect. Each defect opportunity must be independent of the others. Defect sequences that are conditional on the occurrence of an initial defect are considered together as a single defect opportunity.

defects per unit (DPU)
An estimated number of defects observed at the end of the production process (or upon customer delivery) when the exact number of opportunities is unknown. The estimate is based on the number of defects found during inspection.

Design for Six Sigma (DFSS)
A methodology for designing new processes, products, or services or completely redesigning ones that already exist to achieve 3.4 defects per million opportunities or less.

design of experiments (DOE)
A methodology that involves the investigation of factors whose variation might impact the output of a work process. It is used to enhance the predictability of a process.

DMADV
An innovation process that ensures that an organization's products, processes, or services consistently meet current customer requirements. The term DMADV is an acronym for the process's five sequential steps: Define, Measure, Analyze, Design, and Verify.

DMAIC
Six Sigma's rigorous approach for statistical problem solving. The term DMAIC is an acronym for the process's five sequential steps: Define, Measure, Analyze, Improve, and Control.

entitlement
The best performance results obtainable without adding more resources.

Failure Mode and Effects Analysis (FMEA)
A method of identifying specific ways in which a product, process, or service might fail and developing countermeasures for those failures.

fault tree analysis (FTA)
A tool for evaluating a process's design, operation, and reliability. All factors affecting the process's success or failure are placed in a single diagram for evaluation.

5S workplace streamlining
A lean-enterprise method of creating a clean and orderly workplace that exposes waste and errors. The term 5S stands for Sort, Shine, Set in Order, Standardize, and Sustain.

flowchart
A block diagram that illustrates the sequential actions and decisions that represent the steps of a process. It might follow a logical, geographical, physical, or functional means to break a process down into smaller steps or activity increments.

Function Analysis System Technique (FAST)
A mapping technique that graphically depicts work processes and products and identifies function dependencies.

Gantt chart
A program-planning method used to indicate the projected start and completion times for scheduled activities of a project. Its horizontal bars show which tasks can be done simultaneously over the life of the project.

hidden factory
A part of a process that adds no value for the customer and involves fixing things that weren't done right the first time.

just-in-time delivery (JIT)
To deliver a product exactly when it is needed at the quality level required. JIT reduces required inventory levels.

kanban system
A production-control system that uses cards or tickets as visual signals to trigger or control the flow of materials or parts during the manufacturing process.

Kano analysis
A tool for classifying and prioritizing customer needs. It enables a company to rank requirements for different customers to determine which are most important.

key process input variable (KPIV)
A performance indicator that describes in-process performance of work in progress or identifies the performance contribution of suppliers to internal work processes. (See *process X.*)

key process output variable (KPOV)
A performance indicator describing key business-results areas from an external view-point outside the organization. (See *business Y.*)

line of sight
A linked and aligned performance-relationship structure that enables executives to see how front-line workers deliver the company strategy and permits front-line workers to understand how their activities deliver the company strategy.

measurement systems analysis (MSA)
The study of an organization's measurement system to determine its reliability. An improperly functioning measurement system can introduce variability that negatively impacts process capability.

MECE analysis
A $y = f(x)$ analysis where the top-level metrics provide an operating definition for sustained success, and these metrics cascade to actionable measures with local accountability. The term *MECE* stands for mutually exclusive, completely exhaustive. The breadth is mutually exclusive, with no logical overlaps, and the depth is completely exhaustive, with no missing considerations.

multi-vari analysis
A method of identifying patterns of variation within a work process.

non-value-added
Activities or tasks performed during the production of a product or service that do not contribute to meeting customer requirements. Their elimination from the work process does not degrade its overall performance or results.

Pareto chart
A chart that ranks problems by their relative frequency or importance to help a team focus on causes that offer the greatest potential for improvement if solved.

Plan-Do-Check-Act (PDCA) Cycle
A structured, systematic approach for developing and implementing actions of any type. The first step is to plan for action by collecting and analyzing data and developing alternatives. The second step is to implement the selected alternative on a small scale to pilot the change. The third step is to evaluate the results and compare them with expected values. The fourth step is to adopt the change if the desired results were achieved.

poka-yoke
The discipline of applying simple, low-cost methods to either prevent mistakes or detect them immediately and request a corrective action before the mistakes can be repeated and the defects passed on to customers.

problem statement
A succinct statement that describes what the problem is, where and when it occurs, potential reasons why it occurs, how the process operates at the point of the problem, and who is involved in the problem or in a potential solution.

process average
The central tendency of a given process characteristic across a given amount of time or a specific point in time.

process capability
A ratio of the "voice of the process" to the "voice of the customer" that measures the process variability relative to the customer specification and the nominal or target value for performance. This ratio relates customer requirements to actual process performance (see *Cp* and *Cpk*).

process model
A block diagram that illustrates the flow of a work or business process and illustrates the boundaries of the process, its major inputs, and outcomes delivered. It might be broken down from the process level to the activity level and perhaps further broken down to the task level.

process X
An indicator of performance for a work process. It is an independent variable in the equation $y = f(x)$.

Pugh matrix
A tool that helps determine which potential solutions are more desirable than others. All solutions are evaluated in terms of their strengths and weaknesses and then assigned scores. This tool is usually associated with the QFD method.

quality function deployment (QFD)
A methodology for aligning the design of an organization's products and services with the expectations of its customers.

realization review
An assessment of the financial benefits realized after a protracted implementation phase of a Six Sigma project. It is done to ensure that the project's anticipated benefits were realized and whether they transferred to the bottom line.

Recognize step
The step in the Six Sigma analysis process during which an organization's top-level managers determine the strategic issues the organization faces and prioritize the selection of improvement projects.

road map
A time-sequenced program for introducing future product or process developments. It indicates what will be developed and when it is targeted for delivery.

rolled throughput yield (RTY)
A process to determine the probability that a product will make it through a multi-step process correctly the first time it is produced or that a process will work correctly each time it is used.

root-cause analysis
The process of identifying sources of variation to identify the key sources causing a problem. Eliminating these root causes will make the biggest impact toward solving the problem.

SIPOC
A diagram that enables a team to develop a high-level understanding of a process under study, including the upstream and downstream links. The term *SIPOC* stands for Suppliers, Inputs, Process, Outputs, and Customers.

SMED
A method of reducing the time required for setups and changeovers of production machinery so that these operations do not interfere with continuous workflow or productivity. This technique was developed by Shigeo Shingo as part of the Toyota Production System. The term *SMED* stands for Single Minute Exchange of Dies.

standard deviation
A statistical indicator of variability, dispersion, or spread of values in a statistical distribution.

statistical process control (SPC)
The application of statistical methods and procedures relative to a process and a given set of performance standards.

storyboard
A graphical summary of the progress of a project and the methodology used. It is used to track data, decisions, and actions and to create a pictorial record of an improvement project.

stratification
The separation of data into subsets that share similar characteristics.

SWOT analysis
A planning device for capturing all the factors that a leadership team needs to consider as they plot their organization's strategic direction. The term *SWOT* stands for strengths, weaknesses, opportunities, and threats.

systematic innovation process (SIP)
A process used to engage teams in a structured approach to innovation by applying appropriate tools in a facilitated process.

Theory O
A style of management where decisions are based on opinion and anecdotal information rather than validated by objective facts.

Theory X
A style of management where decisions are dictated by management without input, feedback, or challenge from other members of the organization.

Theory Y
A style of management where decisions are made with the participation of an entire group and each group member has an opportunity to make his/her personal opinion heard. Also called consensus management.

tollgate review
A method of reviewing progress and checking key deliverables at the completion of each step of the DMAIC and DMADV processes.

total cycle time (TCT)
The total elapsed time from customer-need identification to delivery of a product, from new-product design concept to cost-effective production, or from identification of a new business opportunity to stable operations.

total productive maintenance (TPM)
A process that ensures every piece of equipment used in a production process is always able to perform its required tasks so that production is never interrupted due to equipment failure.

trend analysis
The use of a run chart to study observed data for a process-performance measure over a period of time in an effort to see trends or patterns in its real-time behavior.

TRIZ
A systematic approach for creating innovative solutions to technical problems. It is especially useful for new product development, service delivery, and solving production problems.

value-added

Activities or tasks performed during the production of a product or service that increase its value to the customer.

variation

Any quantifiable difference between individual measurements. Such differences can be classified as being due to either common causes (i.e., random) or special causes (i.e., assignable).

voice of the customer (VOC) analysis

A method for identifying the key drivers of customer satisfaction. This enables an organization to effectively design, deliver, and improve its products and services.

Work-Out

A group decision process conducted in a constrained workshop. A cross-functional team meets and develops a defined position based on solid data analysis and recommends a course of action. A team of managers listens to the presentation, challenges the team on assumptions, data analysis, and logic, and then either makes a firm yes or no decision or sets a date for the decision to be made after requesting additional data to drive a conclusion.

$\overline{X}$ & R Chart

A type of control chart that displays variability in the process average and range across time and represents the process's capability over time.

y = f (x)

A formula that enables an organization to identify key process drivers and determine what factors in a process can be changed to improve the CTQs.

yield

The percentage of production output that is in conformance with the specification. Can be calculated as a first-pass yield (the percentage of product that goes through production without rework) or rolled throughput yield (the probability that a product will be produced right the first time).

zero defects

A long-range concept that implies the end state of a never-ending improvement process. It is viewed as the achievement of Six Sigma–quality performance.

About the Author

Gregory H. Watson is president and managing partner of Business Systems Solutions, Inc. He was inducted into the International Academy for Quality in 1997 and currently serves as its Secretary/Treasurer. Mr. Watson is a past president and fellow of the American Society for Quality (ASQ), companion of the Institute for Quality Assurance in the U.K., and a fellow of the Australian Organization for Quality, the Quality Society of AustralAsia, and the World Productivity Science Council.

He was awarded the 2001 ASQ Lancaster Medal in recognition of his global efforts in extending the body of quality knowledge and the 2001 Association for Quality & Participation (AQP) President's Award in recognition of his career contributions to the quality profession. Also in 2001, Mr. Watson delivered a fiftieth-anniversary Deming lecture to the Japanese Union of Scientists and Engineers. In 2000 he was named one of the global "twenty-one voices of quality in the twenty-first century" by *Quality Progress* magazine.

Since 1993, Mr. Watson has provided executive quality-consulting services to some of the world's leading firms, including American Express, DuPont, ExxonMobil, Ford, Gemplus, Hewlett-Packard, Johnson Controls, Monsanto, Nokia, STMicroelectronics, and Toshiba. He can be contacted at gregbss@aol.com.

Process-Sigma Conversion Table

Yield	DPMO	Process Sigma	Yield	DPMO	Process Sigma
99.9999%	1	6.27	92.00%	80,000	2.91
99.9997%	3	6.04	91.00%	90,000	2.84
99.9990%	10	5.77	90.00%	100,000	2.78
99.99%	100	5.22	85.00%	150,000	2.54
99.90%	1,000	4.59	80.00%	200,000	2.34
99.80%	2,000	4.38	75.00%	250,000	2.17
99.70%	3,000	4.25	70.00%	300,000	2.02
99.60%	4,000	4.15	65.00%	350,000	1.89
99.50%	5,000	4.08	60.00%	400,000	1.75
99.40%	6,000	4.01	55.00%	450,000	1.63
99.30%	7,000	3.96	50.00%	500,000	1.50
99.20%	8,000	3.91	45.00%	550,000	1.37
99.10%	9,000	3.87	40.00%	600,000	1.25
99.00%	10,000	3.83	35.00%	650,000	1.11
98.00%	20,000	3.55	30.00%	700,000	0.98
97.00%	30,000	3.38	25.00%	750,000	0.83
96.00%	40,000	3.25	20.00%	800,000	0.66
95.00%	50,000	3.14	15.00%	850,000	0.46
94.00%	60,000	3.05	10.00%	900,000	0.22
93.00%	70,000	2.98			

Yield Conversion Table

Sigma	DPMO	Yield	Sigma	DPMO	Yield
6	3.4	99.99966%	2.9	80,757	91.9%
5.9	5.4	99.99946%	2.8	96,801	90.3%
5.8	8.5	99.99915%	2.7	115,070	88.5%
5.7	13	99.99866%	2.6	135,666	86.4%
5.6	21	99.9979%	2.5	158,655	84.1%
5.5	32	99.9968%	2.4	184,060	81.6%
5.4	48	99.9952%	2.3	211,855	78.8%
5.3	72	99.9928%	2.2	241,964	75.8%
5.2	108	99.9892%	2.1	274,253	72.6%
5.1	159	99.984%	2	308,538	69.1%
5	233	99.977%	1.9	344,578	65.5%
4.9	337	99.966%	1.8	382,089	61.8%
4.8	403	99.952%	1.7	420,740	57.9%
4.7	687	99.931%	1.6	460,172	54.0%
4.6	968	99.90%	1.5	500,000	50.0%
4.5	1,350	99.87%	1.4	539,828	46.0%
4.4	1,866	99.81%	1.3	579,260	42.1%
4.3	2,555	99.74%	1.2	617,911	38.2%
4.2	3,467	99.65%	1.1	655,422	34.5%
4.1	4,661	99.53%	1	691,462	30.9%
4	6,210	99.38%	0.9	725,747	27.4%
3.9	8,198	99.18%	0.8	758,036	24.2%
3.8	10,724	98.9%	0.7	788,145	21.2%
3.7	13,903	98.6%	0.6	815,940	18.4%
3.6	17,864	98.2%	0.5	841,345	15.9%
3.5	22,750	97.7%	0.4	864,334	13.6%
3.4	28,716	97.1%	0.3	884,930	11.5%
3.3	35,930	96.4%	0.2	903,199	9.7%
3.2	44,565	95.5%	0.1	919,243	8.1%
3.1	54,799	94.5%			
3	66,807	93.3%			

Additional publications to help you with your Six Sigma Initiative...

GOAL/QPC

The Lean Enterprise Memory Jogger™

Competitiveness in the new economy demands streamlined operations and a total organizational effort to improve bottom-line performance from shop floor to boardroom. This book provides quick access to lean principles and practices with comprehensive "how-to-do-it" guidance on the goals of the lean enterprise, visual management, error proofing, the Kanban system, and more (see complete chapter list below). **Code 1077E**

- Introduction to lean concepts
- The goals of the lean enterprise
- Visual management
- Mapping the value stream
- Error proofing
- Quick changeover
- Standard operations
- One-piece flow
- The Kanban system
- Lean metrics
- Total productive maintenance

Project Management Memory Jogger™

This pocket guide is the most cost-effective way to ensure that your project teams achieve high-quality results. It provides every member of your organization with an easy-to-use road map for managing all types of projects. Whether your team is planning the construction of a new facility or implementing a customer feedback system, this pocket guide helps you avoid typical problems and pitfalls and create successful project outcomes every time. It is packed with useful information on everything from project concept to completion. The method described in the *Project Management Memory Jogger™* is consistent with industry standard approaches such as PMBOK, with an emphasis on participation, empowerment, individual accountability, and bottom-line project results. It utilizes tools and concepts from continuous process improvement and applies them to make project management something that is accessible to all teams working on projects. **Code 1035E**

The Black Belt Memory Jogger™

Provides new and experienced Black Belts and others with guidance on their roles, and contains tips and step-by-step instructions for using over twenty-one advanced tools. Starting with the DMAIC model, *The Black Belt Memory Jogger™* offers plenty of Six Sigma know-how. Use this book as a training tool or as a quick reference to keep your teams and projects on track. **Code 1075E**

The Design for Six Sigma Memory Jogger™

Based on the Define-Measure-Analyze-Design-Verify (DMADV) methodology, *The Design for Six Sigma Memory Jogger™* guides you, step-by-step, through the design process and clearly and concisely presents tools for:

- Identifying the voice of the customer
- Prioritizing Critical to Quality characteristics
- Creating high-level and detailed design elements
- Assessing risks
- Testing designs
- Validating process capability

Code 1078E

The Six Sigma Memory Jogger II™

A portable teaching and reference guide for everyone in the organization, *The Six Sigma Memory Jogger™ II* explains the what, why, and how of Six Sigma. It provides a Six Sigma overview, explains the DMAIC process, and offers detailed instruction on how to perform over forty Six Sigma analytical, decision-making, and planning tools. This pocket guide provides a concise and convenient source of everything your team needs to succeed. **Code 1076E**